W9-BJQ-159

# F Is for FRANCE

ALSO BY PIU EATWELL

*They Eat Horses, Don't They?:*
*The Truth About the French*

# F Is for FRANCE

## A CURIOUS CABINET OF FRENCH WONDERS

## Piu Eatwell

Thomas Dunne Books
St. Martin's Press
New York

THOMAS DUNNE BOOKS.
An imprint of St. Martin's Press.

F IS FOR FRANCE. Copyright © 2016 by Piu Eatwell.
All rights reserved. Printed in the United States of
America. For information, address St. Martin's Press,
175 Fifth Avenue, New York, N.Y. 10010.

www.thomasdunnebooks.com
www.stmartins.com

The Library of Congress Cataloging-in-Publication Data
is available upon request.

ISBN 978-1-250-08773-7 (hardcover)
ISBN 978-1-250-08774-4 (e-book)

Our books may be purchased in bulk for promotional,
educational, or business use. Please contact your
local bookseller or the Macmillan Corporate
and Premium Sales Department at
1-800-221-7945, extension 5442, or by e-mail at
MacmillanSpecialMarkets@macmillan.com.

First Edition: June 2016

10  9  8  7  6  5  4  3  2  1

For my husband, Nikolaï,
to commemorate ten years
of adventure in Gaul

# F Is for FRANCE

# Introduction

Of the many themed trivia books out in the bookshops today, there is a noticeable gap, a silence that seems all the more remarkable the more one reflects upon it. That is, there is no miscellany or book of trivia dedicated to France and the French.

This omission seems all the more glaring in that France—above almost any other country—is replete with arcane laws and bizarre paradoxes. What is more, it is often through these details of peculiar historical incident or quirky custom that we learn the most about our Gallic neighbors and allies. The same could be said of the people of any other country. Are the unique words of different languages telling: the fact that there is a word in Japanese (*karoshi*) for death from overwork, and in Brazilian Portuguese (*cafuné*) for the act of tenderly running your fingers through the hair of one you love? Such words and phrases, unique to the language, exist in French, too: for example, the noun *serein*, signifying the clear, light rain that falls at sunset after a beautiful day.

The purpose and joy of trivia and miscellany books are precisely that they revel in supposedly insignificant minutiae. They prove that there is, as Hamlet said, special providence "in the fall of a sparrow." Moreover, a book celebrating the delicious variety and vagaries of French culture seems all the more apposite today, when that very culture itself has been the subject of recent terrorist and ideological attack. To adopt and espouse everything fun and French has now become, to a degree, a political stance, as the popular Twitter hashtag *#jesuisenterrasse* has shown. To sit on a café terrace and drink wine is no longer an act of French frivolity, but rather of cultural defiance.

With this in mind, therefore, and with the considered reflections of an Anglophone who has now lived for a decade in France, I offer the following as a tribute to everything eccentrically, paradoxically, surprisingly, and delightfully French.

# A Is for...

## ...Absinthe

⚜ Absinthe, an iconic drink intimately linked to the French cafés of the Left Bank, is a highly alcoholic beverage derived from the flowers and leaves of the herb known as *Artemisia absinthium* (or "grand wormwood").[1] It also contains green anise, sweet fennel, and—the key to its mind-bending properties—the chemical thujone. It is usually a bright green color, hence its popular name, the "green muse" or *la fée verte* ("green fairy"). Absinthe is traditionally drunk diluted with water, with the addition of sugar.

Elaborate rituals have developed around the preparation and consumption of absinthe, involving special glasses and perforated spoons to permit the mixing of water and sugar as they are added to the drink:

### The Proper Way to Prepare Absinthe in Polite Society

1. Pour a quantity of absinthe into the glass, amounting to about one-fifth of the total capacity (1 to 1½ ounces is common).

2. Place the absinthe spoon across the glass, with the notch in the spoon resting on the rim of the glass. Place a sugar cube in the spoon.

3. Slowly drizzle a steady volume of water over the sugar cube, allowing the cube to become saturated first, until the glass is full or according to taste.

4. Close your eyes and await the approach of the green fairy.

*Recipe from the Wormwood Society*

---

Absinthe was hugely popular from the 1860s onward in France and continental Europe, so much so that the hour between five and six p.m. was called *l'heure verte* in bars and cafés. It was the muse of the poet Baudelaire, and the lurid colors of Van Gogh's paintings have been attributed to the psychedelic influence of the drink. Edgar Degas's 1873 painting *L'absinthe* epitomizes the loneliness and drugged haze of the absinthe drinker in the popular imagination. One detractor observed:

> Absinthe makes you crazy and criminal, provokes epilepsy and tuberculosis, and has killed thousands of French people. It makes a ferocious beast of man, a martyr of woman, and a degenerate of the infant, it disorganizes and ruins the family and menaces the future of the country.

Absinthe was thus associated with social disorder, degeneracy, and crime. The reputation of absinthe reached such a low

## Nineteenth-Century Absinthe Recipe

| | |
|---|---|
| Grande wormwood, dried and cleaned | 2.5 kilograms |
| Hyssop flower, dried | 500 grams |
| Citronated Melissa, dried | 500 grams |
| Green anise, crushed | 2 kilograms |
| Alcohol (85 proof) | 16 liters |

Infuse the entire cucurbit for 24 hours, add 15 liters of water, and distill carefully to produce 15 liters of product, adding:

| | |
|---|---|
| Alcohol (85 proof) | 40 liters |
| Ordinary water | 45 liters |

Produces 100 liters at 45 degrees; mix and let rest.

Translated from *Traité de la Fabrication des Liqueurs*, 1882[2]

point that it was banned in most Western countries in the early twentieth century, including the United States in 1912 and France in 1915. In the United States, absinthe was banned until 2007 (the French ban was not lifted until 2011).

♛ Recent years, however, have seen an absinthe revival, with the arrival of new brands boasting names evocative of the drink's bohemian origins, such as La Fée Absinthe or the Australian brand Moulin Rooz.

## ...Adultery

♕ The French have traditionally been famed for their tolerance of adultery by those in public office, especially with regard to their presidents. Perhaps the most famous case of publicly tolerated adultery was that of President François Mitterrand, who had a whole secret family, unbeknownst to the French public. The secret was only revealed after the president's death in 1996, when his lover, Anne Pingeot, and their daughter, Mazarine, appeared at his grave. The French public was disgusted—not so much at the president's behavior, but rather at the press, for revealing details of his private life.

♕ *Cinq à sept* ("five to seven p.m.") was the phrase used to describe the hours when married French couples would traditionally cheat on their spouses. In the days when writers such as Victor Hugo kept an entire establishment for their mistress, the *cinq à sept* was the time for discreet liaisons, before a gentleman would set off back home for dinner with his wife. By the late twentieth century, however, all that had changed. "In Paris, no one makes love in the evening anymore; everyone is too tired," sighs a character in Françoise Sagan's 1966 novel *La Chamade*. Nowadays, the term *cinq à sept* is more likely to be used in the Quebeçois sense, of "happy hour" at the bar.[3]

♕ Under French law, infidelity can be "intellectual" as well as physical. In other words, excessive smoking, playing too much soccer, spending too much time with the local bishop, and phone sex can all be grounds for divorce. In 1986, a French court granted a divorce to a husband on the grounds of the "intellectual infidelity" of his wife. The reason for the divorce was that the wife had allowed a rival to assume intellectual precedence in her thoughts over her husband, thus giving her husband the impression that she considered him worthless.[4]

## ...Animals

⚜ Contrary to their reputation for indifference to animals, the French can be extraordinarily caring to them. In the Breton village of Saint-Léger-des-Prés, for example, it is illegal to slander donkeys by the use of such insulting terminology as "jackass," "dumb as an ass," etc. Anybody breaking this law is required to make amends by offering apologies in the form of carrots or sugar lumps to the donkeys residing within the boundaries of the commune. The law was introduced in 1991 by the then mayor of Saint-Léger-des-Prés, who was inordinately fond of donkeys. He cited, in support of the law, the French author Chateaubriand: "We impugn the name of the ass with a thousand idiocies, unworthy of comparison to him."[5]

⚜ In the town of Granville in northwestern France, elephants are banned on the beach. The ban dates from 2009, when local circuses came to the town and visiting pachyderms were taken for a stroll on the beach, with the predictable resultant deposits. Circus organizers were irate at the time the ban was introduced, claiming that the public were being prevented from getting a closer look at the animals, and that the beach had been polluted anyway by more offensive chemical emissions.[6]

⚜ The national animal symbol of France is the rooster.

⚜ The French own the most pets of any country in Europe,

with 36.4 million goldfish, 10.7 million cats, and 7.8 million dogs. Twenty-five percent of French households own a dog and 27 percent own a cat.[7]

☫ The most popular breed of dog in France is not the French bulldog—as one might expect—but the German shepherd.[8]

☫ In the course of divorce hearings in France, the custody of pets is a frequent cause of dispute. French law does not allow shared custody of pets or the alternating of weekends, and judges have traditionally taken a dim view of having to arbitrate over the future of furry and feathered friends. So much so that, when a judge in Rouen was asked to rule on who would have custody of the couple's dog, he replied curtly that he was not prepared to do so, given that the "dog was perfectly capable of deciding the issue for itself."[9]

☫ Being historically a farming country, France still has a lot of rules on the books relating to farm animals. For example, the law states that if your chickens run into your neighbor's coop and lay their eggs there, they belong to the owner of the land and you have no right to the eggs—that is, unless the credulous fowl have been lured over the boundary by "fraud or artifice."[10]

☫ There is a confirmed population of wild kangaroos living near the village of Émancé in the forest of Rambouillet, west of Paris. Apparently, the gray marsupials escaped an animal park in the 1970s, and their descendants are now bounding happily along the forest paths in the wild. The feral kangaroos are so much a part of the local scene that there are signs signaling their presence, and the magazine of the school in Émancé is called *The Joking Kangaroo*.[11]

☫ The Great Cat Massacre is the name given to a bizarre

incident that occurred in Paris during the 1730s. A group of apprentices at a printing press on rue Saint-Séverin resented the fact that their master and mistress treated their cats better than the apprentices themselves. The cats were spoiled and pampered, while the apprentices were beaten, mistreated, exposed to freezing weather, and fed scraps from the table, which even the cats wouldn't eat. In order to exact revenge, therefore, one of the apprentices mimicked the sound of a cat yowling through the night. The master and mistress, desperate to be rid of the noise, ordered the cats to be rounded up and killed. The apprentices caught the cats and beat them half to death; they then held a "mock trial," found the cats guilty of witchcraft, and sentenced them to death by hanging. Various explanations for this stunning case of animal cruelty have been put forth by historians, including the theory that the action by the apprentices represents an early example of worker revolt.[12]

꧁ The first public zoo in Paris, the Ménagerie du Jardin des Plantes, was created in 1794, during the time of the French Revolution. This resulted from the demands of the National Assembly that all privately owned exotic animals be donated to the menagerie or stuffed. During the time of the Paris commune, many of the animals were eaten by besieged Parisians. The Ménagerie is the second most ancient zoological park in the world.[13]

꧁ The Zoo de Pessac near Bordeaux was once home to the only documented case of a jealous hippo. The founder of the zoo, Jean Ducuing, kept a pet hippo called Komir as the zoo's star attraction. Komir and Ducuing were more or less inseparable: they played together every day, and posters for the zoo showed Ducuing with his head in the hippo's enormous open mouth. The trouble started, however, when Ducuing got himself a new toy—a tractor—and started playing with that instead. After months of being ignored, Komir threw a fit. When Ducuing cycled past the hippo's enclosure one day and ignored him, he stampeded through the electric fence and charged at his neglectful master. Ducuing, of course, didn't stand a chance with four tons of jealous hippo on him. His widow took over the zoo, and questions as to what to do with Komir were tactfully settled when the hippo himself died from ingesting a rubber ball six months later. The circumstances were not regarded as suspicious.[14]

## …Architecture

The gracious façades of central Paris owe their existence to one Georges-Eugène Haussmann (1809–1891), commonly known as Baron Haussmann. Haussmann was drafted by Emperor Napoleon III to completely reconstruct the city, with new parks, squares, and boulevards. A graduate of the famous Collège Henri IV and Lycée Condorcet of Paris, he set about laying out the outlines of the modern city as we know it: major

stations to connect Paris to the rest of France (Gare de Lyon and Gare du Nord), grand boulevards and sweeping squares, and large parks to the north, south, east, and west (the Bois de Boulogne, Bois de Vincennes, Parc des Buttes-Chaumont, and Parc Montsouris). Parisians, however, grew tired of the incessant building and rebuilding, and complained about the drain on the city's coffers. Eventually forced to resign by Napoleon, Baron Haussmann spent his last days focusing on his massive, three-volume *Mémoires*. He died quietly in Paris in 1891, at the age of 82.[15]

🐚 The famous art nouveau entrances to the Métro stations of Paris are largely the creations of the eccentric French architect Hector Guimard (1867–1942). They have been described by one critic in these terms:

> Constructed like the Crystal Palace out of interchangeable, prefabricated cast-iron and glass parts, Guimard created his métro system in opposition to the ruling taste of French classical culture . . . Guimard's system flourished, emerging overnight like the manifestation of some organic force, its sinuous green cast-iron tentacles erupting from the subterranean labyrinth to support a variety of barriers, pergolas, maps, hooded light fittings and glazed canopies. These surrealistic "dragonfly's wings"—to quote a contemporary critic—received a mixed, not to say chauvinistic, press, the verdigris color of their iron supports being regarded as German rather than French.[16]

Unfortunately, Guimard was never truly appreciated in his day. He emigrated to New York where he eventually died as a virtually forgotten figure. On his death, his widow even offered the *hôtel particulier* in which the couple had lived as a gift to the city of Paris, but was refused. Many of his creations have now, however, been reconstructed or restored—a belated recognition of this hugely important, if eccentric, architect.

⚜ The exquisite glass and cast-iron canopies extending above many hotel, Métro, and theater entrances in Paris and other French cities are called *marquises*. Appearing as an architectural feature at the end of the nineteenth and early twentieth centuries, the *marquises* signaled a relaxation of the rather austere aesthetic of Baron Haussmann. The word *marquise* was originally used to signify a tentlike structure outside an entrance to keep out the rain, and today's *marquises* combine practicality and grace with the same purpose in mind.[17]

# B Is for...

## ...Baguette

☙ There are more bakeries in Paris (1,784) than bars (1,124).[18]

☙ The French consume about 10 billion baguettes a year—that, is about 320 baguettes per second.[19]

☙ A true French baguette may contain only pure flour without additives, although water, yeast, and salt are allowed. Eggs, milk, and oil are never used. Baguettes must be baked in a stone furnace at a minimum of 482°F for 25 minutes.[20]

☙ For the past twenty years, the City of Paris has awarded a prize for the Best Baguette of the Year. In order to compete, entries must measure between 22 and 26 inches, weigh between 9 and 11 ounces, and contain 0.6 ounces of salt for every 2 pounds of flour. Baguettes entered into the competition are identified by number only, to guarantee anonymity. The criteria for assessment include texture, taste, and smell, scored on a scale of 0 to 4. The *boulangerie* that makes the winning baguette has the honor of supplying the president at the Élysée Palace for a year. The 2015 *prix de la meilleure baguette de Paris* went to the artisan *boulanger* Djibril Bodian, whose *boulangerie*, Le Grenier à Pain, nestles in the shadow of the Sacré-Coeur at 38, rue des Abbesses, in the picturesque district of Montmartre.[21]

## ...Beef

♔ *Steak frites* (steak and fries) is a French bistro classic, voted in a recent poll of French people as the fifth most popular dish in France.[22]

♔ Historically, the traditional French cut of beef was the *rumsteak* (rump steak), although nowadays the *entrecôte* (rib steak) is the more popular cut.

♔ Steak can be asked for as *bleu* (virtually raw), *saignant/ à point* (medium-rare), or *bien cuit* (well-done—a *cuisson* that a native French person will never ask for, and which is reserved for Anglophone foreigners).

### American and French beef cuts compared

American and French beef cuts can be compared as follows:

The main difference between American and French cuts is how certain areas are subdivided, with French butchery manifesting both a more complex division and the French willingness to eat more or less everything, including parts of the animal (tongue, cheeks, tail) that would be considered unsavory by the

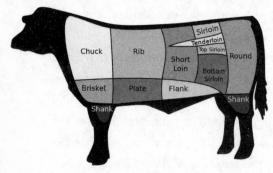

*American beef cuts*

average American. Tenderloin is *filet de boeuf*, and sirloin *faux-filet*. Other more exotic French cuts include *paleron* (a piece of shoulder used for braising), the *pavé* or *filet de rumsteak*, the *onglet* (tenderloin), and the *bavette* (skirt steak).[23]

*French beef cuts*

## ...Beret

☖ The beret, quintessentially French headgear, originated in the southwest of France, where it was worn by peasants and sold commercially from the seventeenth century onward.

☖ The traditional French beret is made with half a mile of merino wool, and has a ring of leather inside to help it fit snugly on the head. It is waterproof, resistant to ultraviolet light, and keeps its shape even after being rolled.[24]

☖ These days, berets are rarely worn in French cities, and are seen mainly in rural areas. Only one traditional beret manufacturing firm remains in France.[25]

☖ The main market in the world for berets today is the military, with the French army, United Nations, and NATO still using the traditional cloth cap. The U.S. army stopped using cloth berets in 2011, replacing them with patrol caps.[26]

⚜ The image of the archetypal Frenchman in a beret, riding a bicycle with a string of onions, comes from the Breton fishermen who came to Britain from the nineteenth century onward, to sell their onions door to door. The English called them "Onion Johnnies" due to the fact that many of them were called *Jean* (the French version of John), and for many English people, this was as close to France or the French as they would ever get. The cross-Channel trade died out in the latter half of the twentieth century, although the image of the "Onion Johnny" lived on as a clichéd symbol of a Frenchman.[27]

⚜ The beret was once the signature headgear of the film director. Great directors of art cinema such as Ingmar Bergman and Luis Buñuel wore a beret on set when shooting, to signal their status as artists, as did the American director Billy Wilder. The film director Francis Ford Coppola continues the tradition of wearing a beret on set, to symbolize his independence from mainstream commercial cinema.

⚜ The beret was replaced as the traditional headgear of film directors in the 1980s by director Steven Spielberg, who popularized the baseball cap as a new badge for the moviemaker. Since baseball is both quintessentially American and a mass spectator sport, the transformation of the director's crown from beret to baseball cap seemed to underline the triumph of mass-market, popular American cinema over its French-inspired, art house rival. Today, the standard uniform of a film director of any nationality is a baseball cap, jeans, and sneakers.

## ...Brains, etc.

☝ Many traditional French delicacies are considered by Anglophone folk to be downright bizarre, even revolting. Apart from the notorious snails and frogs' legs (see Snails; Frogs), these include:

- *Fromage de tête* (literally "head cheese"): a type of French terrine made of meat from the head of a cow or calf, traditionally preserved in jelly or aspic. The parts of the head used vary, but the brain, ears, and eyes are generally removed.*
- *Tetines* (cows' udders): traditionally fried, these were in the past particularly associated with Franco-Jewish cuisine.
- *Andouillette* (pigs' intestines): a delicacy of Lyon.
- *Boudin noir* (literally, "black pudding"—a form of blood sausage): the best place to savor this is the town of Mortagne au Perche in Normandy, which has a special boudin festival in March, including a competition to see who can eat the most (up to three miles of boudin are regularly consumed). Proceedings are monitored with an eagle eye by the Confrérie des Chevaliers du Goûte-Boudin ("Fraternity of the Knights of the Blood-Sausage Tasters").[28]

---

*"Head cheese" is not to be confused with the term *Cheeseheads*, used to denote someone from Wisconsin, now more specifically referring to fans of the Green Bay Packers.

## Recipe for Making 1 Ton of Boudin Noir

116 gallons blood

143 pounds fat

65 sets of cleaned pigs' intestines (or "hog casings")
   and string

32 gallons milk

1,080 eggs

242 pounds spinach

143 pounds onions

24 gallons cream

Heat the ingredients in an *extremely large* pan. Stuff the hog casings and tie with string. Poach in barely bubbling water.[29]

♕ Alexandre Dumas (1802–1870)* is better known as the author of swashbuckling novels of high adventure, including *The Three Musketeers* and *The Count of Monte Cristo*, than as a gourmet with a penchant for bizarre cuisine. He was, however, a great adventurer in the realms of all that is weird and wonderful in food. His *Grand dictionnaire de cuisine* was published posthumously in 1873, and includes exotic recipes for everything from wolf to bear. Here, for example, is Dumas' recipe for elephant:

---

*The Alexandre Dumas of *The Three Musketeers* fame is referred to by the French as *Alexandre Dumas, père*, to distinguish him from his son, *Alexandre Dumas, fils*, who was also a well-known writer.

## A Recipe for Elephants' Feet from Alexandre Dumas

*Vietnam is perhaps the only country today that eats elephant flesh, and considers it a great delicacy. When the King kills one for his table, he sends chunks of it to the great and the good, a mark of the greatest honor; but the most highly esteemed parts are always the trunk and feet. Levaillant says that it is an exquisite dish: "grilled elephants' feet," he states, "are the food of Kings; I could never have thought that an animal so heavy, so dense, could provide such a delicate dish; I would have no trouble devouring the foot of my elephant."*

*We will therefore give, for those of our readers who would like to follow Levaillant, a recipe for elephants' feet, which we owe to Monsieur Duglerez of the House of Rothschild:*

*Take one or several young elephants' feet, and remove the skin and bones after soaking them for about four hours in warm water. Divide them into four pieces lengthways and cut them in two, then blanch them for fifteen minutes in water. Run them in cold water and drain them on a serviette. Take a heavy saucepan with a tightly fitting lid; place at the bottom two slices of Bayonne ham, set the elephants' feet on top, then four onions, a head of garlic, some Indian spices, a half-bottle of Madeira, and three spoonsful of stock. Cover the pan tightly and simmer for ten hours. Remove the*

> *fat; add a glass of port and 50 small green pimentos*
> *blanched in boiling water, to preserve their color. The*
> *sauce should be well-flavored and very sharp; make*
> *sure of this last point.*
>
> *Le Grand dictionnaire de cuisine*
> by Alexandre Dumas (1873)

☙ The most bizarre period of French cuisine took place during the Siege of Paris, from 1870–1871, in the course of the Franco-Prussian war. At this time, Parisians were cut off from their normal food supplies. Extreme alternatives followed. Horses quickly found themselves on the best menus in Parisian clubs, followed by cats, dogs, and rats. Finally, in desperation, people resorted to the animals of the Paris zoo: camels, kangaroos, and even the famous zoo elephants, Castor and Pollux, found themselves on restaurant plates. A menu of the Parisian Café Voisin on Christmas Day 1870, the ninety-ninth day of the siege, reads as follows:

### Hors-D'Oeuvres:
Butter, Radish, Stuffed Donkey's Head
Sardines

### Soups:
Red Bean Soup with Croûtons
Elephant Consommé

**Entrées:**
Roasted Camel à l'Anglaise with Fried Goujons
Jugged Kangaroo
Roasted Side of Bear with Pepper Sauce

**Main Courses:**
Roasted Leg of Wolf with Venison Sauce
Cat Surrounded by Rats
Watercress Salad

Antelope Terrine with Truffles
Bordeaux Mushrooms
Buttered Peas

**Dessert:**
Rice Pudding with Jam

**Cheese:**
Gruyère

Despite his very Gallic-sounding name, the journalist and politician Henry Du Pré Labouchere (1831–1912) was in fact English. He was in Paris at the time of the Prussian siege and kept a diary of events. Here he describes the exotic diet of Parisians at the time:

All the animals in the Zoological Gardens have been killed except the monkeys; these are kept alive from a vague and Darwinian notion that they are our relatives, or at least the relatives of some of the members of the Government, to whom in the matter of beauty nature has not been bountiful . . .

In the rue Blanche there is a butcher who sells dogs, cats, and rats. He has many customers, but it is amusing to see them sneak into the shop after carefully looking round to make sure that none of their acquaintances are near. A prejudice has arisen against rats, because the doctors say that their flesh is full of trichinae. I own for my part I have a guilty feeling when I eat dog, the friend of man. I had a slice of a spaniel the other day, it was by no means bad, something like lamb, but I felt like a cannibal. Epicures in dog flesh tell me that poodle is by far the best, and recommend me to avoid bulldog, which is coarse and tasteless.

Diary of the Besieged Resident in Paris by Henri
Du Pré Labouchere, 1871.

# C Is for...

## ...Cabaret

☙ The most famous Parisian cabaret, the Moulin Rouge, opened in 1889—the same year as Paris's Exhibition Universelle, which featured the Eiffel Tower.

When the Moulin Rouge first opened, it featured a garden with enormous statues, including a giant elephant, whose belly housed an Arabian-themed gentleman's club complete with a stage for exotic dancers and an opium den. Gentleman would enter the elephant through the leg and climb the staircase to the stage. The Paris vice squad also made the elephant's belly its headquarters for a time, as an ideal viewpoint from which to survey the goings-on at the nightclub.[30]

☙ A little-known *noir* side to the Paris cabaret scene also existed. Only streets away from the glitz and razzmatazz of the Moulin Rouge were the so-called "dark cabarets." They included Le Cabaret du Néant ("The Cabaret of Nothingness"), where habitués dined at tables made from coffins, and drank absinthe from cups that were replicas of human skulls; La Taverne du Bagne ("The Tavern of Exile"), designed to represent the interior of a prison, with iron bars and waiters dressed as convicts, dragging balls and chains; and L'Enfer ("Hell"), where guests were greeted by paintings of nude women and a door in the shape of an enormous, cavernous mouth, waiting to devour them—a preview of the delights to come that evening. The doorman at L'Enfer famously greeted guests with the salutation "Enter and be damned!" The waiters also dressed as devils, and an order for three black coffees spiked with cognac was relayed to the kitchen as: "Three seething bumpers of molten sins, with a dash of brimstone intensifier!" A wit with a decidedly existential sense of humor even set up a rival nightclub next door to L'Enfer called Le Ciel ("Heaven"). Sadly, after the Great War, the dark cabarets became obsolete, possibly because the general public had by then experienced enough of the gloomy side of life, and wanted to lighten up a little.[31]

## …Catacombs

The city of Paris perches on top of a warren of some 170 miles of underground passages and tunnels, which have been home to the remains of 6 million Parisians since the 1700s. These passages—known as the catacombs—have drawn a number of myths and stories around themselves. One of the strangest is the legend of Philibert Aspairt, said to have been a doorkeeper at the Val-de-Grâce hospital, who disappeared into the catacombs in 1793. Aspairt, so the story goes, was looking for the cellars of the Carthusian convent, in order to steal a couple of bottles of their famed chartreuse. He was never seen again; eleven years later, in 1804, his body is said to have been discovered in the catacombs, recognizable by the hospital keys that still hung from his belt. A tomb in his memory was erected in the catacombs and stands there to this day. Whether Aspairt was a real person or an urban myth remains uncertain, but a piece of evidence tending to support the truth of the story is a death certificate in the city archives in the name of "Philibert Asper," dated May 2, 1804.[32]

Only a tightly restricted section of the catacombs is open to the public. The remainder is strictly off limits, but that has not stopped a hardy group of adventurers—the *cataphiles*—from exploring their depths. In 2004, police patrolling the underground passages found an entire theater with seating concealed in a vast 4,300-square-foot cave under the chic 16th arrondissement, equipped with a bar, pressure cooker for making couscous, stock of '50s noir films, and contemporary cave paintings on the walls. When the police returned later with electricians to investigate the power source, they found that the lines had been cut, and a note had been left that read "Do not try to find us." The exploits of the *cataphiles* are just the latest in a long line of clandestine catacomb events: in 1897, the underground tunnels played host to a secret concert given by nearly fifty members of the Paris Opera. There are many tribes and groups of *cataphiles,* and they even have their own patron saint. This is not a Christian saint, however, but none other than the spectral doorkeeper who met his death in the catacombs, Philibert Aspairt himself, whose ghost is said to still wander the dank underground passageways.[33]

## ...Champagne

There are many sparkling wines produced around the world, but only very few are permitted the name of Champagne. In order to be validly called Champagne, a sparkling wine must meet three criteria:

- It must be made from one of three varieties of grape (Pinot Noir, Pinot Meunier, or Chardonnay).
- The grapes must come from the Champagne region of France.
- The wine must be produced by a specific method, known as the *méthode champenoise.*[34]

♕ The provocative Anglo-American journalist and literary critic Christopher Hitchens once stated, "The four most over-rated things in life are Champagne, lobster, anal sex, and picnics."[35]

♕ According to a recent survey, the most popular world brand of Champagne is Moët & Chandon. No less than 2,415,900 9-liter cases of this famous brand were consumed in 2013.

---

### The Top Ten Champagne Brands for 2013 by Worldwide Volume Sales are as Follows:

| | |
|---|---|
| 1. Moët & Chandon | 6. Taittinger |
| 2. Veuve Clicquot | 7. Piper-Heidsieck |
| 3. Nicolas Feuillatte | 8. Pommery |
| 4. G. H. Mumm | 9. Lanson |
| 5. Laurent-Perrier | 10. Canard-Duchêne[36] |

Interestingly, only one of the top ten *world* sellers in Champagne brands—Veuve Clicquot—makes the top three list of those favored by the French. The Champagne preferred by the country that invented it is a much less well-known brand: Ruinart, the oldest Champagne house in France. Founded by Nicolas Ruinart in the city of Reims, Ruinart has been produced constantly and exclusively since 1729. The house was inspired by the foresight of a seventeenth-century Benedictine monk, Dom Ruinart, who realized that the newly invented "wine with bubbles," then popular with aristocrats, had a promising future. Ruinart is followed in the French ratings, in equal second position, by the ubiquitous Veuve Clicquot and another lesser-known brand loved by connoisseurs, Roederer.[37]

🥂 Veuve Clicquot ("Widow Clicquot") is named after Barbe-Nicole Ponsardin, the widow of François Clicquot, son of the founder of the Champagne house. She was the first woman to take over a major Champagne house.

🥂 In the movies, James Bond drinks Champagne more than any other drink (thirty-five occasions in twenty-two films). 007's preferred choice of fizz is (perhaps predictably) the brand favored by the British upper class, Bollinger, followed by Dom Pérignon.[38]

🥂 Legend has it that the classic Champagne glass or "coupe" was adapted from a wax mold of the left breast of Marie-Antoinette. The rather more likely—albeit prosaic—theory is that the coupe was designed for sparkling wine in England around 1663, and thus predated both Champagne and Marie-Antoinette by almost a century. The story inspired the sculptor Jane McAdam Freud to design a Champagne coupe molded on the fashion model Kate Moss's left breast, for the celebration of the model's twenty-five years in the business in 2014.[39]

♛ There are 49 million bubbles in a standard-size bottle of Champagne. The finer the Champagne, the smaller the bubbles, which can mean over 60 million bubbles for the finest vintage bubbly.[40]

♛ Champagne corks are impossible to put back in a bottle after opening as they are greatly constricted, and inserted by machine to withhold the 90-pound-per-square-inch pressure (three times the pressure of a car tire). The velocity at which a cork leaves the bottle is around 50 mph. The record holder for distance traveled by a Champagne cork is currently held by the American Heinrich Medicus, who managed to achieve a distance of 177 feet 9 inches in 1988.[41]

♛ Collectors of the metal plaques wired onto the corks of Champagne bottles, which can be of great value, are called placomusophiles.[42]

♛ The actress Marilyn Monroe is said to have taken a bath in 350 bottles of Champagne. Whether this story is true or not, the actress was certainly a fan of fizz: her room was permanently littered with bottles of the finest, and her favorite vintage was Dom Pérignon 1953.[43]

♛ As a special Valentine's Day promotion in 2012, the Cadogan Hotel in London offered "Champagne baths." Guests could choose to have their baths filled with vintage Louis de Custine for £4,000, Perrier-Jouët for £6,000, Perrier-Jouët Rosé for £8,000, or vintage Dom Pérignon for £25,000. The most popular choice was the Dom Pérignon.[44]

♛ There are fourteen sizes of Champagne bottle. The smallest is the Piccolo (quarter bottle/187 ml), and the largest is the

Melchizedek (40 bottles/30l). Only about twenty bottles of Melchizedek size are produced a year, and they are made specially to order. The sizes and popular names of Champagne bottles are as follows:

| Type | Capacity | Bottle Equivalent | Number of Glasses |
|------|----------|-------------------|-------------------|
| Piccolo | 18.75 cl | 1/4 | 1 |
| Demi | 37.5 cl | 1/2 | 3 |
| Bottle | 75 cl | 1 | 6 |
| Magnum | 1.5 l | 2 | 12 |
| Jeroboam | 3 l | 4 | 24 |
| Rehoboam | 4.5 l | 6 | 36 |
| Methuselah | 6 l | 8 | 48 |
| Salmanazar | 9 l | 12 | 72 |
| Balthazar | 12 l | 16 | 96 |
| Nebuchadnezzar | 15 l | 20 | 120 |
| Solomon | 18 l | 24 | 144 |
| Sovereign | 25 l | 34 | 200 |
| Primat | 27 l | 36 | 216 |
| Melchizedek | 30 l | 40 | 240[45] |

🥂 Champagne is generally bottled in dark green or black bottles, as just sixty minutes under artificial lighting or daylight in a clear-glass bottle is liable to generate "light-struck" aromas, ruining the wine. However, one of the most famous and expensive Champagnes in the world—Cristal by Louis Roederer—is sold in clear glass bottles. The reason lies in the Champagne's regal origins. Cristal was originally produced in 1876, exclusively for Tsar Alexander II of Russia. The Tsar— with some justification—was terrified of the prospect of assassination, and so wished his bottles of Champagne to have flat bottoms and be made of clear glass, so they could be checked for poison. Cristal is now one of the most exclusive Champagnes on the planet. It is still made to the original specifications: a transparent flat-bottomed lead crystal bottle, with a gold label, and golden foil. Common methods of circumventing the risk of spoilage are to store the wine in a dark cellar, closed fridge, or wrapped in dark cellophane.[46]

## ...Cheese

♛ Contrary to popular belief, the French are *not* the biggest world consumers of cheese. This award goes to the feta-loving Greeks, who consume an impressive 68 pounds of cheese per person per year. Nevertheless, the French still consume a lot of cheese: 57 pounds a year (compared to 33 pounds for the average American and 24 pounds for the average Briton).[47]

♛ There are close to one thousand varieties of cheese in France, many of which are protected by the AOP label (*Appellation d'origine protégée*), a European food label designed to protect foodstuffs with a distinct gastronomic and cultural heritage.

♛ The only French cheese to be eaten with a spoon is Vacherin Mont d'Or, to which King Louis XV was said to be especially partial. The cheese is made once a year between August 15 and March 15. It derives its unique, nutty taste from the spruce bark in which it is wrapped. Only eleven factories in the French Jura region are licensed to produce it.[48]

☙ After scientific analysis by electronic "noses"—that is, machines equipped with special sensors to detect different chemical aromas—the world's smelliest cheese has been officially pronounced as Vieux Boulogne, a soft cheese from northern France. The particularly pungent smell of this cheese is believed to be a result of the beer in which it is washed during the production process, reacting with the cheese. At the time of the announcement, there was some surprise that the laurel for the world's smelliest cheese did not go to Époisses de Bourgogne, a cheese so pungent that an urban myth has developed that it is banned from public transportation in Paris.[49]

☙ The French custom is for cheese to be served as the penultimate course *before* dessert (or instead of it), not *after,* as in Britain, or as an appetizer, as in America. Cheese in France is generally served with bread and fruit or fruit preserves, not biscuits or crackers. Traditionally, one cow's-milk, one goat's-milk, and one sheep's-milk cheese are served. Cheese will be presented in the center of the table, typically accompanied by a crisp white wine such as Riesling, or a light red such as Beaujolais.[50]

## The Top Ten Most Popular Cheeses In France Are:[51]

1. *Camembert*: the classic creamy cows'-milk cheese from Normandy.

2. *Goat cheese*: low-fat soft cheese with a tart, earthy flavor, popular in salads and quiches.

3. *Brebis Basque*: sheep's-milk cheese from the Basque region, traditionally eaten with a preserve of black cherries.

4. *Comté*: hard cheese traditionally made from unpasteurized cows' milk, from the Franche-Comté region of France.

5. *Grated Emmental*: yellow, medium-hard cheese that originated in Switzerland and is the standard French cooking cheese in grated form.

6. *Saint-Nectaire*: soft cow's-milk cheese from the Auvergne region.

7. *Cantal*: firm cheese from the Cantal region; one of the oldest cheeses in France, which graced the table of King Louis XIV.

8. *Whole Emmental*: Emmental in ungrated form.

9. *Reblochon*: soft cheese from the Savoy region of the Alps. The name derives from the Savoyard verb *reblocher*, meaning "to pinch a cow's udder again" (the cheese originally being made from the second milking).

10. *Roquefort*: France's most famous blue cheese, a salty, tangy creation often called the *roi*, or king, of French cheeses.

## ...Chef

The French word *chef* derives from the Latin word *caput* (meaning "head"). In French, however, *chef* is not limited to the field of cuisine, and can mean the head of a business or a political or religious leader.[52]

꙳ In French restaurant kitchens, the chef heads the *brigade de cuisine*, a complex hierarchy of cooks dedicated to different tasks, which was developed by the great French chef Georges-Auguste Escoffier. The hierarchy includes the *chef, sous-chef,* and a host of lesser roles encompassing everything from the *saucier* (sauce maker) to the *poissonnier* (fish cook) and the *potager* (soup cook).[53]

꙳ At least two top French chefs have committed suicide rather than face culinary disgrace. François Vatel, chef to the Prince of Condé, was placed in charge of a great feast at the Château de Chantilly in 1671 to honor King Louis XIV. When the fish ordered for the banquet failed to turn up on time, he ran on his sword rather than face the humiliation of the guests missing a course. Centuries later, in February 2003, the top chef Bernard Loiseau committed suicide with a shot-gun, rather than face the prospect of losing a Michelin star.[54]

## ...Children

꙳ The French birthrate, at 2.01 children per woman on average, is—along with that of Ireland—one of the highest in Europe.[55]

꙳ The French state awards a medal—*la Médaille d'honneur de la Famille Française*—to families with the most children. A bronze medal is awarded to the mother who has raised, in worthy fashion, four or five children; silver for six or seven; and gold for eight or more.[56]

꙳ French courts are much stricter with regard to the names that can be given to children than those in England or America. In 1993, existing laws preventing parents from freely choosing their child's name were modified, but a name can still be forbidden by the courts if it would be "against the child's interests" or expose them to ridicule. Thus, in 2015, courts in Valenciennes in northern France forbade a couple from naming their child Fraise (strawberry), and another couple from calling their baby girl Nutella. In 2013, a boy named Jihad caught the notice of school authorities when the three-year-old was seen wearing a T-shirt emblazoned with the words "I am a bomb" on the front, and his name and date of birth, 9/11, on the back. His mother was acquitted of supporting terrorism by a court in Avignon.[57]

---

### The Top Ten Girls' Names in France in 2015 Were:

| | |
|---|---|
| 1. Emma | 6. Manon |
| 2. Lola | 7. Jade |
| 3. Chloé | 8. Louise |
| 4. Inès | 9. Léna |
| 5. Léa | 10. Lina |

---

### The Top Ten Boys' Names in France in 2015 Were:

| | |
|---|---|
| 1. Nathan | 6. Enzo |
| 2. Lucas | 7. Louis |
| 3. Léo | 8. Raphaël |
| 4. Gabriel | 9. Arthur |
| 5. Timéo | 10. Hugo |

*L'Officiel des prénoms* (éd. First)

## ...Cigarette

☙ Over a quarter of the French population are daily smokers. This is fewer than the world's heaviest smoking country, Greece (more than 30 percent). However, it is higher than the British (22 percent) and the Americans (16 percent). Almost 25 percent of French teenagers ages 15 to 19 smoke, and the average age of exposure to cigarettes in France is a rather shocking 11 years old.[58]

☙ Nicotine was named after the Frenchman Jean Nicot (1530–1600), a diplomat and scholar who introduced the tobacco plant to France in 1559, from Portugal. Tobacco had long been smoked by Native Americans prior to its discovery in Europe, partly for its mind-bending psychedelic properties. Believing that tobacco had curative effects, Nicot sent some tobacco powder to Catherine de' Medici in 1560 after a visit to Portugal, to treat the terrible migraines of her son, the frail and sickly child-king François II. The treatment was initially successful; tobacco was baptized the "queen's herb" and subsequently licensed for sale in apothecaries.[59]

☙ The modern French film that holds the record for the most smoking scenes is *Gainsbourg: Vie héroïque* (2010), a life of the French poet and songwriter Serge Gainsbourg, directed by Joann Sfar. The film clocks in with no less than 43 minutes of continuous smoking time.[60]

## ...Coffee

**The basic types of French coffee offered in cafés and restaurants are as follows:**

- *Café/Café Noir/Espresso/Express*: a shot of espresso, often very dark and bitter
- *Café Allongé*: espresso diluted with water
- *Double/Double express*: a double shot of espresso
- *Filtré*: filtered coffee, also known as *café américain*
- *Noisette*: an espresso with a spot of cream. Its name, French for "hazelnut," is derived from its color.

- *Café crème*: milky coffee— rarely ordered by French people, most often asked for by foreigners

🐚 The *cafetière*, or so-called "French press" coffeemaker, is something of a misnomer. It was probably invented by an Italian, Attilio Calimani, who patented it in 1929. In any event, the French rarely use the French press to make coffee these days, being generally addicted to Nespresso machines.[61]

🐚 One of the most famous poems in the French language, "Déjeuner du matin" by Jacques Prévert, recounts being dumped by someone over a cup of coffee and a cigarette.

🐚 The nineteenth-century French novelist Honoré de Balzac was addicted to coffee, which he consumed in great quantities to fuel his prodigious literary output. He always had a pot of the strongest black brew simmering on the stove, and was rumored to drink up to fifty cups of coffee per day (although this fact has never been definitively proven). Balzac even wrote a eulogy in praise of the inspirational power of coffee in an article entitled "The Pleasures and Pains of Coffee," published in the 1830s. In this, he states: "Coffee is a great power in my life; I have observed its effects on an epic scale. Coffee roasts your insides." He goes on to prescribe a harsh, and decidedly risky, method for using the most potent brew to keep inspiration from flagging:

> Finally, I have discovered a horrible, rather brutal method that I recommend only to men of excessive vigor . . . It is a question of using finely pulverized, dense coffee . . . consumed on an empty stomach . . . From that moment on, everything becomes agitated. Ideas quick-march into motion like battalions of a grand army to its legendary fighting ground, and the battle rages. Memories charge in, bright flags on high; the cavalry of metaphor deploys with a magnificent gallop; the artillery of logic rushes up with clattering wagons and cartridges; on imagination's orders, sharpshooters sight and fire; forms and shapes and characters rear up; the paper is spread with ink—for the nightly labor begins and ends with torrents of this black water, as a battle opens and concludes with black powder.

According to Balzac, consuming coffee this potent has the result that "you will fall into horrible sweats, suffer feebleness of the nerves, and undergo episodes of severe drowsiness." But for a writer who had set himself the task of completing the ninety-novel series *La Comédie humaine* (*The Human Comedy*), this was perhaps a necessary price to pay in order to stay awake long enough to complete his work.[62]

&#9752; Contrary to common belief, it appears that modern Parisians do not while away the hours sipping endless cups of *café noir* while pontificating about philosophy on the terrace of their local bistro. Neither the French nor Americans even make it into the top ten of world coffee consumers, a list dominated by the countries of Scandinavia and Eastern Europe. The per capita consumption of the top coffee-consuming country—the Netherlands, at 2.4 cups per day—is almost the same as those of the United States, United Kingdom, Spain, and France combined. In a 2010 review of the writer Stieg Larsson's hit Swedish crime series, the Millennium Trilogy, *The New York Times* wrote incredulously about how the days seemed to revolve around endless cups of coffee:

> Everyone works fervidly into the night and swills tons of coffee; hardly a page goes by without someone "switching on the coffee machine," ordering "coffee and a sandwich" or responding affirmatively to the offer "Coffee?"[63]

Little did the newspaper know how true to life Larsson had been, as a recent survey shows:

## The World's Biggest Coffee Drinkers
*Coffee consumption per capita*

| Country | Cups per day |
| --- | --- |
| Netherlands | 2.414 |
| Finland | 1.848 |
| Sweden | 1.357 |
| Denmark | 1.237 |
| Germany | 1.231 |
| Slovakia | 1.201 |
| Serbia | 1.188 |
| Czech Republic | 1.17 |
| Poland | 1.152 |
| Norway | 1.128 |
| Slovenia | 1.076 |
| Canada | 1.009 |
| Belgium | .0981 |
| Switzerland | .971 |
| New Zealand | .939 |
| USA | .931 |
| Austria | .803 |
| Costa Rica | .793 |
| Greece | .782 |
| Algeria | .765 |
| Macedonia | .755 |
| France | .694 |

*Euromonitor International, 2014.*

## ...Cuisine

♔ French cuisine has been inscribed in UNESCO's List of the Intangible Cultural Heritage of Humanity. Other items in the extensive and somewhat eclectic list include:

- Albanian Folk Iso-Polyphony
- Argentine Tango
- Austrian Viennese Coffee House Culture
- Flamenco Dancing from Spain
- Korean Tightrope Walking
- The Mediterranean Diet
- Mongolian Knuckle-Bone Shooting
- The Panama Hat from Ecuador[64]

♔ The favorite dish of French people is—perhaps surprisingly—not a classic of French cuisine, but the universally popular world dish, roast chicken. This is followed closely by more recognizably French signature dishes, *magret de canard* (duck breast), and in third place, the *plateau de fruits de mer* (traditional seafood platter). The full list, according to a 2015 study by pollster BVA, is as follows:

### 15 Most Popular Dishes in France

1. *Poulet rôti (roast chicken): 20.3%*

2. *Magret de canard (duck breast): 20.2%*

3. *Plateau de fruits de mer (seafood platter): 19.9%*

4. *Blanquette de veau (veal in white sauce): 19%*

5. *Steak frites (steak and fries): 17.8%*

6. *Boeuf bourguignon (traditional beef stew): 14.4%*

7. *Pot-au-feu (traditional chicken stew): 13.5%*

8. *Couscous: 11.7%*

9. *Choucroute (sauerkraut): 11.6%*

10. *Gratin dauphinois (potato gratin): 10.4%*

11. *Spaghetti à la bolognaise: 9.6%*

12. *Tartiflette (potato,cheese and bacon hash): 9.6%*

13. *Lasagnes: 9%*

14. *Paëlla: 6.8%*

15. *Cassoulet (casserole of white beans, meat, and vegetables): 8.7%*

*French polling company, BVA, February 2015*

The foreign cuisine that French people like best is Italian, followed by Chinese, and then Japanese, a particular favorite with the younger generation. Young people preferred Japanese cuisine, while older people favored Chinese.[65]

According to a 2010 survey, travelers voted France as the country with the most overrated cuisine.[66]

Contrary to the worldwide reputation of French cuisine, the culinary capital of the world was Tokyo, according to the 2015 Michelin Guide. The Japanese capital held on to its top spot from the previous year, boasting more Michelin-starred restaurants than any other capital in the world.[67]

A large number of foods and dishes are named after famous French people. They include:

- *Pommes/Potatoes Anna*: a casserole of sliced potatoes cooked in butter, created and named by French chef Adolphe Dugléré after the nineteenth-century courtesan Anna Deslions, who hung out at the Café Anglais.[68]
- *Béarnaise sauce*: believed to originate in the nickname of the French king Henry IV (1553–1610), known as "*le Grand Béarnaise*." It was invented by the chef at the hotel Pavillon Henri IV at Saint-Germain-en-Laye, who, when asked what the name of the sauce was, invented a name as his glance fell on a bust of the king in the room.[69]
- *Oeufs/Eggs Berlioz*: The French composer Hector Berlioz (1803–1869) is the inspiration for this dish of soft-boiled eggs.[70]
- *Chateaubriand*: A cut and a recipe for steak named for François-René-Auguste de Chateaubriand (1768–1848), French writer and diplomat.[71]
- *Poulet/Chicken sauté George Sand*: George Sand was the pseudonym of the French writer Amantine-Aurore-Lucile Dupin Dudevant (1804–1876). She was a colorful figure in mid-nineteenth-century Parisian salons, and there are several dishes named after her, including this one.[72]
- *Saucisse/Sausage Jésus*: These small sausages of the French Basque and Savoy regions have lofty aspirations, as their nomenclature implies. There is also a type of sausage known as the Baby Jésus de Lyon, so-called

because the pig skin in which the sausage is stuffed makes it resemble a swaddled baby.[73]

- *Truite/Trout Jeanne d'Arc*: Perhaps not the most flattering dish by which the French warrior and martyr Joan of Arc (1412–1431) is remembered.[74]

- *Sole Jules Verne*: The celebrated French novelist Jules Verne (1828–1905) has several dishes named after him including this, a sauce, a garnish, grenades of turkey, and partridge. Which is perhaps appropriate, as he regularly mentioned entire menus in his books.[75]

- *Cotelettes d'agneau/Lamb chops Victor Hugo*: The celebrated French writer, Victor Hugo (1802–1885), is commemorated with these.[76]

# D Is for...

## ...Death

♛ In France, it is possible with the permission of the president, to marry a dead person. Posthumous marriage originated in the 1950s, when the fiancée of a man killed after a dam burst in the town of Fréjus applied to the then president, Charles de Gaulle, to carry through the couple's marriage plans and was granted permission. Since then, applications have been made and have succeeded at various times, for posthumous marriage under this law.[77]

♛ In the village of Sarpourenx, in the Pyrénées-Atlantiques, it is forbidden to die in the commune if one does not have a plot in the local cemetery. The local law was passed in 2008 as a result of restrictions on expansion of the village burial ground. Similar laws have been passed in the towns of Le Lavandou and Cugnaux.[78]

♛ France is a country of memorable deathbed utterances. Famous last (French) words include:

• "You will not find me alive at sunrise."—Michel de Nostredame or Nostradamus (1503–1566), world-famous seer and prophet: last words and final prediction.[79]

- "I am about to—or I am going to—die: either expression is correct."—Dominique Bouhours (1628–1702), French grammarian.[80]

- "Why do you weep? Did you think I would live forever?"—Louis XIV (1638–1715), King of France, also known as the "Sun King": died after a reign of seventy-two years, the longest documented reign of any European monarch.[81]

- "I feel nothing, apart from a certain difficulty in continuing to exist."—Bernard de Fontenelle (1657–1757), French philosopher.[82]

- "This is no time to make new enemies."—Voltaire (1694–1778), French philosopher, when asked to reject Satan on his deathbed.[83]

- "Do not forget to show my head to the people, it is well worth seeing."—Georges Jacques Danton (1759–1794), leading French revolutionary executed by guillotine.[84]

- "Oh Liberty, what crimes are committed in thy name!"—Marie-Jeanne Roland, or Madame Roland (1754–1793), French revolutionary executed by guillotine.[85]

- "Aim true! France forever! Fire!"—Michel Ney, known as Marshal Ney (1769–1815), a commander during the French Revolutionary and Napoleonic Wars. Executed by firing squad, he refused to wear a blindfold and was granted the right to give the order to fire.[86]

- "A King should die standing."—Louis XVIII (1755–1824), King of France.[87]

- "Nurse, it was I who discovered that leeches have red

blood."—Baron Georges Cuvier (1769–1832), French naturalist and zoologist.[88]

- "Doctor, do you think it could have been the sausage?"—Paul Claudel (1868–1955), French poet.[89]
- "This time it will be a long one."—Georges Clemenceau (1841–1929), French statesman.[90]
- "All the damn fool things you do in life you pay for."—Edith Piaf (1915–1963), French singer celebrated for songs such as *"Non, je ne regrette rien."*[91]

And, to add a few words of deathbed wisdom from foreign expatriates who died in France:

- "What is the answer? In that case, what is the question?"—Gertrude Stein (1874–1946), American writer who made Paris her lifelong home.[92]
- "Oh, you young people act like old men. You are no fun."—Josephine Baker (1906–1975), African American dancer notorious for shocking the world by dancing topless in a skirt of banana skins. Baker was reportedly attempting to seduce a man several decades younger than her when she died of a heart attack later that night.[93]

[See also: Marie-Antoinette, under *Queen*; Napoleon; Mata Hari].

♛ The manner of death of a number of famous French personages is no less singular than their deathbed utterances. Take, for example:

- Philippe, son of Louis VI of France (1116–1131): Met his death after a pig ran under his horse in a Paris market, causing the horse to stumble.[94]
- Charles VIII of France (1470–1498): While conducting his queen into a tennis court, struck his head against a lintel, which caused his death.[95]
- Gabrielle d'Estrées or "la Belle Gabrielle," mistress of Henri IV (1573–1599): died from eating an orange.*[96]
- Jean-Baptiste Lully, French composer (1632–1687): hit himself on the big toe with his own conductor's baton while conducting a performance of his *Te Deum*. He refused to have the toe amputated, and gangrene developed.[97]
- Julien Offray de la Mettrie, French doctor and philosopher (1709–1751): died from acute indigestion after eating too much truffle pâté at a feast.[98]
- Nicolas Gilbert, French poet (1750–1780): died after swallowing a key during a fit of insanity.[99]

[See also: Isadora Duncan, and François Vatel, under *Chef*].

♛ The word *necrophilia* (defined as a "sexual attraction to corpses") was first used in relation to a Frenchman. The term was coined by the Belgian psychiatrist Joseph Guislain and first used in connection with the crimes of François Bertrand (1824–1850), a sergeant in the French army who was also known as the "Vampire of Montparnasse." In the late 1840s,

---

*The long-held belief was that Gabrielle was poisoned; however, modern explanations have posited puerperal fever (eclampsia) as the cause of her death.

Bertrand dug up a series of human bodies from the famous Parisian graveyard at Montparnasse in order to copulate with them. He was eventually captured in the cemetery and sentenced to a year in prison, the prosecution failing to establish rape (which can only be committed on a living person). He was released in 1850 and committed suicide soon after. The story of François Bertrand inspired the American writer and screenwriter Guy Endore to write his 1933 horror novel *The Werewolf of Paris*, in which the character of the werewolf is called Bertrand. The novel was a number-one *New York Times* bestseller on publication, and is still considered the founding book of werewolf literature (on a par with Bram Stoker's *Dracula* in relation to vampire writing).[100]

# E Is for...

## ...Eiffel Tower

☗ The Eiffel Tower was originally intended as a temporary structure. It was designed for the 1889 Paris Exhibition by the engineer Gustave Eiffel, who guaranteed when it was built that it would last for twenty years.[101]

☗ During its construction, there was a public outcry that the Eiffel Tower violated principles of good taste and marred the Paris skyline. A petition published by the French newspaper *Le Temps* read:

> We, writers, painters, sculptors, architects and passionate devotees of the hitherto untouched beauty of Paris, protest with all our strength, with all our indignation in the name of slighted French taste, against the erection . . . of this useless and monstrous Eiffel Tower . . . To bring our arguments home, imagine for a moment a giddy, ridiculous tower dominating Paris like a gigantic black smokestack, crushing under its barbaric bulk Notre Dame, the Tour

Saint-Jacques, the Louvre, the Dome of Les Invalides, the Arc de Triomphe . . . all of our humiliated monuments will disappear in this ghastly dream. And for twenty years . . . we shall see stretching like a blot of ink the hateful shadow of the hateful column of bolted sheet metal.[102]

The writer Guy de Maupassant is said to have lunched in the Tower daily, because that was the only spot in Paris from which it could not be seen.

♛ Once finished in 1889, the Eiffel Tower surpassed the Washington Monument to assume the title of the tallest man-made structure in the world (986 feet). It had to yield this title in 1930 to the Chrysler Building in New York City (1,057 feet). Later that year a radio antenna was added to the Tower to make it taller, but this victory was short-lived.[103]

♛ The Eiffel Tower has the highest number of suicides of any French landmark (although safety nets have helped reduce the number): on average, about four people per year.[104]

The Eiffel Tower ranks fifth in world suicide sites.

---

### The Top Ten World Suicide Sites are:

1. Golden Gate Bridge, San Francisco, USA

2. Niagara Falls, Ontario, Canada

3. Prince Edward Viaduct, Ontario, Canada

4. Clifton Bridge, Bristol, England

5. Eiffel Tower, Paris, France

6. Jacques Cartier Bridge, Montreal, Canada

7. Beachy Head, Eastbourne, England

8. Coronado Bridge, San Diego, USA

9. Aurora Bridge, Seattle, USA

10. Empire State Building, New York City, USA

*Le Nouvel Observateur, Le triste top 10 des hauts lieux*
*de suicide dans le monde,* 16 Nov. 2012.

The first suicide from the Eiffel Tower occurred in 1898, when a twenty-three-year-old printer's assistant hung himself from one of the beams. He left a note willing his clothes to Gustave Eiffel.[105]

An early accidental death by falling from the Tower was that of a tailor named Franz Reichelt, who in 1912 applied to the Eiffel Tower Company for permission to test a spring-loaded, batwing cape that he had devised and claimed could make him fly. The Company granted permission, but made him sign a disclaimer beforehand. On the appointed day, Reichelt's nerve failed, but taunted by gathered spectators and pressmen, he bravely stepped forth in his cape. Unfortunately, he plummeted straight to the ground, creating a foot-deep hole in the earth below.[106]

A middle-aged man who attempted to leap from the Tower's first level was caught in the nick of time by a guard, who grabbed his leg. He was treated to a free lunch in one of the Tower restaurants to cheer him up, and driven back to his home in the suburbs to ensure that he did not repeat the attempt. The next morning he was found drowned, facedown in one of the duck ponds at the foot of the Tower.[107]

Some stories of attempted suicides from the Tower have happy endings. One day a young woman jumped from the first level but became entangled in the trusswork, enabling her to be rescued. A few months later, she gave birth to a healthy baby boy. Another woman leaped from the first level only to land on the springy roof of a little Renault Dauphine, coming away with merely a ruptured spleen.[108]

⚜ The Eiffel Tower shares the same nickname as that given to the British prime minister Margaret Thatcher—*la Dame de Fer* ("The Iron Lady").

⚜ In 2008, a woman married the Eiffel Tower, changing her name to Erika La Tour Eiffel in honor of her "partner." Erika, an ex-soldier who lived in San Francisco, had a history of "object fetishism," and admitted to a past crush on the Berlin Wall. There are believed to be about forty "objectum-sexual" people in the world, mostly women. Psychiatrists have attributed the condition to a need to exercise control over the object of love.[109]

## ...Etiquette

⚜ French greetings are more formal than American. One is expected to say *bonjour* or *bonsoir* ("good morning" and "good evening") with the honorific title *Monsieur* or *Madame* when entering a shop, and *au revoir* ("good-bye") when leaving.[110]

⚜ In making French introductions, one must introduce

the younger person to an elder, a man to a woman, and the person one knows less well to the person one knows better.

⚜ In France, cutlery is customarily placed *facedown* on the table and not faceup, as in Britain and America. The reason for this practice is said to date from the eighteenth century, when the fashion was for men to have sleeves with extremely expensive embroidered edges; placing the forks faceup would risk catching or tearing the lace. For this reason, forks were placed facedown and, as a consequence, in French aristocratic families, the coat of arms was traditionally engraved on the back, not the front, of forks.[111]

⚜ It is generally considered low-class in France to say *bon appétit* before a meal.[112]

⚜ The knife should be held in the right hand, the fork in the left.[113]

⚜ Salad leaves should not be cut with a knife and fork, but folded with a fork.[114]

⚜ According to French bourgeois etiquette, it is forbidden for a woman to help herself to wine at the table. A desperate female may rattle her glass expectantly, in the hope that the man sitting next to her will notice and oblige.[115]

⚜ In France using a comb, toothpick, or nail clippers in public (indeed, any form of public grooming) is viewed as vulgar. One modern guide to French etiquette remarks: "NEVER apply lipstick at the table: it will give you the bared-teeth appearance of a horny chimpanzee, and also mess up your napkin and the lip of your glass."[116]

⚜ Napkins should be placed on the table after use, but NOT re-folded.[117]

♛ Certain rules of male gallantry still survive among the older generation and upper bourgeoisie in France. They include:

- A man should go into a restaurant first, to ensure the place is not one of ill repute.
- A man should both mount and descend the stairs in front of a woman. This ensures that he does not look at her legs on ascent, and protects her from falling on descent.
- In a restaurant, a man should let the woman take the "banquette" seat, facing the room. Since she can't fill her own glass with wine, he should ensure that hers is always full.
- A man should rise when a woman enters the room.
- In the street, a man should always take the side next to the road, and not next to the wall, which is reserved for the woman.
- A man should wait for a woman to offer her hand before taking it in his own.

# F Is for...

## ...Fashion

☙ The French "Sun King," Louis XIV, had a mania for shoes with red heels, probably to compensate for his short stature. Soon they became a status symbol, and de rigueur for everybody of noble birth: a *pied plat*, or flatfoot, was someone with no social standing.[118]

☙ The first fashion magazine appeared in France in 1672, and was a men's magazine called *Le Mercure Galant*. A female fashion magazine appeared some years later.[119]

☙ The famous Breton-striped shirt—a symbol for many people of the archetypal Frenchman—originated as fishermen's garb and was later adopted as the uniform of the French navy. The original count of stripes was twenty-one, reflecting the number of naval victories of Napoleon. The shirt was spotted by French fashion designer Coco Chanel on a weekend trip to Deauville and transformed into a style icon that has since achieved global recognition, from the perfume bottles of Jean Paul Gaultier to the coats sold by French children's clothing chain Petit Bateau.[120]

☙ The word *denim* comes from the town

of Nîmes in France, and literally means *du Nîmes* ("from Nîmes"). The textile denim originated in Italy and France and spread to the United States when Levi Strauss introduced denim overalls for workers in 1873. By the 1950s, jeans—originally worn by cowboys and miners—had become popular with teenagers of the Beat generation. They have been a staple of fashion ever since. In France, jeans became a hit in the 1960s with an iconic image of Brigitte Bardot on the deck of a cutter off the coast of Saint-Tropez, sporting a pair of denims.[121]

♛ The bikini is a French invention. The first prototype was produced by the French designer Louis Réard in 1946, and sold in a beach shop in Cannes. A designer called Jacques Heim had already created the predecessor of the bikini, a rather heavy two-piece. Réard refined this with a much racier number, consisting of two triangles linked with string on top, and a G-string below. He called his creation the "bikini" after Bikini atoll, a group of islands in the South Pacific where the United States began testing nuclear weapons in the summer of 1946. Réard declared that a bikini was only the real thing if it could be "pulled through a wedding ring," and sold them in matchboxes to prove the point that they were "smaller than the smallest swimsuit." Regular models refused to wear the scandalous outfit, with the result that the bikini was first modeled by a topless cabaret dancer at one of Paris's public swimming pools. It was immediately banned in Italy (where it was declared sinful by the Vatican), Spain, Belgium, and France, and in the United States several women were arrested for sporting the offending garment on beaches.[122]

♛ A famous staple of every woman's wardrobe, the "little

black dress" was a revolutionary design created by French fashion designer Coco Chanel in 1926. Prior to this, black had been traditionally considered a color of mourning. On October 1, 1926, American *Vogue* featured a short, simple black dress decorated with a few diagonal lines. *Vogue* called it "Chanel's Ford"—in other words, like Ford's Model T it was stylish and accessible to women of all classes. *Vogue* quoted Henry Ford's famous dicta that "any customer can have a car painted in any color that he wants so long as it's black," and predicted that the Little Black Dress—or LBD—would become "a sort of uniform for all women of taste." They were right.[123]

♔ The first designer clothes with a logo are said to be the revolutionary tennis shirts designed by French tennis legend René Lacoste in 1933. The signature Lacoste crocodile—always facing left—now graces a range of high-quality sportswear. The claim to be the first designer logo, however, has been challenged by the contention that the "Jantzen Girl" logo (a diving girl in a red swimsuit) was to be seen on swimsuits produced by the Oregon-based firm Jantzen Knitting Mills in the 1920s.[124]

♔ The first miniskirt appeared at a fashion show of French designer André Courrèges in 1965.* It was an A-line skirt that ended just above the knee. While the skirt was greeted in shocked silence by the show's contemporary audience, it soon caught on as epitomizing the free and easy '60s, especially when Mary Quant incorporated it into her "Mod" look at her flagship London store, Bazaar. Quant made Courrèges's original skirt shorter and tighter, and soon the micro-mini had

---

*There is some controversy over the invention of the miniskirt: the British designer Mary Quant has also staked a claim to have invented it.

appeared. Stars like Brigitte Bardot and Twiggy made the look universal, while it became virtually respectable when it was even adopted by the American first lady Jacqueline Kennedy. In other countries, the miniskirt was never really accepted: in South Korea, the fashion police patrolled the streets and measured the length of miniskirts, arresting women whose skirts fell short of regulations.[125]

The bag known as the Birkin is a two-handled leather handbag made by the French fashion house Hermès and named after the Franco-British actress Jane Birkin. The story has it that, in 1981, the chief executive of Hermès, Jean-Louis Dumas, was sitting next to the actress on a flight from Paris to London. She remarked that she had not been able to find a leather weekend bag that she liked. Dumas had a leather bag created for her based on a design that Birkin drew on an airplane sickness bag. Today the Birkin bag has reached iconic status, and at anything from $9,000 to $150,000 in price, is one of the most expensive and coveted handbags in the world. The bag is always made of leather with a matching goatskin lining, with the most expensive option being saltwater crocodile skin. Although it carries no obvious logo, it is immediately recognizable by its rectangular shape and two short, looped handles, and it always carries the Hermès stamp inside. It is produced in irregular quantities at unpredictable times, thus preserving its status of exclusivity. At one point, it had a waiting list of six years—the longest for any bag in history.[126]

The French shoe designer Christian Louboutin is known for his sky-high heels, shoes with his signature shiny red-lacquered soles, and for bringing back the stiletto in the 1990s (his heels have reached 8 inches and higher). However, it is less well known that he also once produced a limited line of blue-soled shoes, so that brides could wear something discreetly blue on their wedding day. Louboutin's biggest client is the author Danielle Steel, who is believed to own over six thousand pairs, and to have bought up to eighty pairs on a single visit to Louboutin's store in Paris.[127]

☝ The French luxury leather goods firm Louis Vuitton destroys unsold merchandise in order to keep up the value of the brand.[128]

☝ The highest-paid French designer is Hubert de Givenchy, who earned an estimated 82 million euros in the year 2014.[129]

☝ A recent survey of French women's favorite lingerie brands came up with some surprising results. The most popular three brands were the practical UK brand Etam, followed by the American brand Victoria's Secret, and then French hosiery giant Dim. Far from slinking around in steamy designer numbers by haute couturiers, French women seem to prioritize comfort and economy over sexiness when it comes to their underwear.[130]

## ...Fast Food

☝ Contrary to popular belief, the French are crazy about fast food. For example:

- The average French person eats about 22 pounds of pizza a year. This puts the French second in the world pizza-eating league, ahead of the Italians and beaten only by the Americans. Ninety-five pizzas are consumed every second in France.[131]

- France is the second-biggest market in the world for McDonald's, after America. Every day, 1.7 million French people eat at McDonald's, and the chain earns over €4.2 billion a year.[132]
- One of the reasons for the huge success of McDonald's in France is the chain's adaptation to local French demands. French McDonald's restaurants were designed so that clients could sit down for a decent period to eat their meal, the chain uses 100% French beef, and its burgers were given specifically French names like the *Charolais* (named after the famous white beef cattle of Burgundy). Not that McDonald's France is unique in this: New Zealand McDonald's have the Kiwi Burger, Uruguay has the McHuevo, India has the lamb-based Maharaja Mac, and Turkey has the spicy Köfte Burger.[133]
- Second to McDonald's in France are the Burger King chain (recently reopened in France) and the Belgian hamburger chain, Quick.

## ...Femme

♛ The world's longest-living human being was a Frenchwoman. Jeanne Louise Calment lived to an incredible 122 years, 164 days. She was born on February 21, 1875 (the year before Alexander Graham Bell got his patent for the very first telephone), and died on August 4, 1997. Many theories were put forward for Calment's extraordinary longevity. They included the fact that she ate more than two pounds of chocolate a week, used to treat her skin with olive oil, rode a bicycle until she was one hundred, and only quit smoking five years before her death. She was also known for a certain tart sense of humor. When somebody took leave by telling her, "Until next year, *perhaps*," she retorted, "I don't see why not! You don't look so bad to me." Another of her many reputed *bons mots* was: "I've never had but one wrinkle, and I'm sitting on it."[134]

꧁ Women in Paris are forbidden to wear trousers, unless riding a bicycle or a horse. The law—which dates from the 1800s—was originally introduced to dissuade the cross-dressing inclinations of the likes

of author George Sand. The law is still, technically, in force. However, in 2013 the French Minister for the Rights of Women stated that it has implicitly been overruled by subsequent legislation putting women on an equal footing with men.[135]

꧁ Women in France were granted the right to vote in 1944 (compared to 1918 in the United Kingdom and 1920 in the United States).[136]

꧁ Until 1964, a Frenchwoman was not allowed to open a bank account, set up a shop, or obtain a passport without her husband's permission.[137]

꧁ A certain number of careers remain closed to females in France. One of the most curious is that women are technically not permitted to be undertakers (a rule that is often broken these days). The ban derives from the fact that undertakers traditionally smashed the toe of a corpse to confirm that the person was indeed dead—a task considered unsuitable for feminine sensibilities.[138]

♛ The first American woman to be awarded France's highest award for gallantry—the *Croix de guerre*—was the African American topless dancer Josephine Baker (1906–1975). Born into poverty to an unmarried mother in St. Louis, Missouri, Baker rose to become a star of the international stage, and made her home in France. But while she is most remembered today for wearing a skirt made of banana skins, there was actually a great deal more to Josephine Baker than topless dancing. She played a key role in the Resistance movement during World War II, and was also a tireless civil rights activist in the 1950s and '60s. In addition to the French Military Cross, she was awarded the Legion of Honor and the Rosette of the Resistance. When she died in 1975, Baker became the first American woman to be buried in France with full military honors.[139]

## ...Films

♛ The only French-born actor to have won a U.S. Academy Award for Best Actor is Jean Dujardin in 2011, for his role in the Oscar-winning silent movie *The Artist*. The French actors Maurice Chevalier, Charles Boyer, and Gérard Depardieu have all been nominated for the award. French actresses have done somewhat better than their male counterparts: the Best Actress honor has been awarded to Claudette Colbert (in 1934, for *It Happened One Night*), Simone Signoret (in 1959, for *Room at the Top*), and Marion Cotillard (in 2007, for *La Vie en Rose*).[140]

♛ Visitors to France will sometimes hear cinema referred to in the French media as the "seventh art." This refers to a definition by the German philosopher Georg Wilhelm Friedrich Hegel (1770–1831), of the "six arts." The Italian film critic Ricciotto Canudo then invented the term *seventh art* in 1911 to describe cinema. The other six arts, as defined by Hegel, are:

- Architecture
- Sculpture
- Painting
- Dance
- Music
- Poetry [141]

☙ According to a 2015 poll, France's favorite film actress is Sophie Marceau (b. 1966). Marceau has a string of hit French films to her credit, although she is probably best known internationally for her roles in *Braveheart* (1995), *Firelight* (1997), and the nineteenth James Bond film, *The World Is Not Enough* (1999).[142]

☙ France's favorite male actor is a comic actor unknown to the English-speaking world, although a huge name in France: Louis de Funès (1914–1983), whose hawk-like features and incredibly mobile facial expressions made him a giant of French cinema and television screens throughout the 1960s and '70s. De Funès famously tussled with a colony of nudists as a bumbling local cop in the hit French television series *Le Gendarme de Saint Tropez*. He also starred in *La Grande Vadrouille* (*The Great Stroll*, 1966), a comedy set in Nazi-occupied France that is one of the highest-grossing French films of all time.[143]

☙ The French public's favorite filmmaker is the director Luc Besson. Besson is celebrated for being a pioneer in the highly

## The Top Ten Highest-Grossing Films in France

1. *Titanic* (1998)

2. *Bienvenue chez les Ch'tis* (2008)*

3. *The Untouchables* (2011)

4. *Snow White and the Seven Dwarfs* (1938)

5. *La Grande Vadrouille* (1966)*

6. *Gone with the Wind* (released in 1950)

7. *Once Upon a Time in the West* (1969)

8. *Avatar* (2009)

9. *The Jungle Book* (1968)

10. *One Hundred and One Dalmatians* (1961)

*J.P.'s Box office, 2015.*

*French comedies

visual and stylized form of cinema known as *Cinéma du look*, at its peak in the 1980s and '90s. His string of international hits include *Subway* (1985), *The Big Blue* (1988), *Nikita* (1990), the sci-fi action film *The Fifth Element* (1997), and *Taken 2* (2012), the second-highest grossing French film in the world, after *The Untouchables* (2011).[144]

☸ Paris's only remaining X-rated cinema is the Beverley Cinema, to be found in rue de la Ville-Neuve in the city's 2nd arrondissement. Here audiences can watch X-rated movies on 35mm film from the 1960s onward, on comfortable red leather sofas. There are regular readings of erotic poetry, and

## The Top Ten Highest-Grossing French Films in the World

1. *The Untouchables* (2011)

2. *Taken 2* (2012)

3. *The Fifth Element* (1997)

4. *Bienvenue chez les Ch'tis* (2008)

5. *Taken* (2008)

6. *Amélie* (2001)

7. *Perfume* (2006)

8. *The Artist* (2011)

9. *Asterix at the Olympic Games* (2008)

10. *March of the Penguins* (2005)

*J.P.'s Box office, 2015*

Thursdays and Saturdays are "couples's nights," when couples can snuggle up to watch a movie, eat popcorn, and do . . . well, whatever . . . The movie theater claims to welcome all who feel alienated from typical "bourgeois" French values.[145]

## ...Fragonard

Most Francophiles and art buffs will have heard of the famous French painter Jean-Honoré Fragonard (1732–1806), he of the naughtily provocative classic rococo painting *The Swing*. Fewer, however, will know that he had a cousin—Honoré

Fragonard—who followed an altogether darker calling. Honoré Fragonard was a celebrated anatomist, and a professor at France's national veterinary school in 1766. His special interest, however, was the skinning and preserving of animal and human specimens by a form of flaying (*écorché*), the precise details of which technique have now been lost. Nevertheless, the Musée Fragonard in Paris's veterinary school still contains a number of eerie *écorchés*, including a llama, goat, three monkeys, two human heads, and three small children. Most grotesque of all are two "sculptures"—a flayed man and an entire horse and rider, fully flayed—presumably intended to replicate a horseman of the Apocalypse.[146]

♔ Fragonard the painter and Fragonard the flayer are not to be confused with the House of Fragonard, one of the most famous French perfume brands, based in the town of Grasse in Provence. Parfumerie Fragonard was established after the Great War by Eugene Fuchs, and is still run by his grandsons. Its classic perfumes are produced according to traditional methods and use only natural ingredients. They are sold in signature, sleek metallic bottles (gold for women and silver for men), to stop the expensive contents from spoiling in sunlight.[147]

[See also: Entry for *Perfume*].


## ...France

♔ The name "France" comes from the Latin *Francia*, which means "land or kingdom of the Franks."[148]

♔ France is the most visited country in the world, with

85 million tourists in 2013. The top-ranking countries for visitors are: 1. France (84.7 million foreign tourists in 2013), 2. United States (69.8 million), 3. Spain (60.7 million), 4. China (55.7 million), and 5. Italy (47.7 million).[149]

☙ The French refer to France as *l'Hexagone* ("The Hexagon") due to its shape, which is roughly that of a hexagon.

☙ France is about the same size as Texas. In fact, Texas is actually slightly larger (268,580 square miles to France's 260,558).[150]

☙ The lowest point in France is the Rhone River Delta, at −13 feet.[151]

France's highest point, also the highest point in Europe, is Mont Blanc, at 15,771 feet high.[152]

☙ France is the fourth most culturally rich country in the world, according to a 2015 UNESCO study. The study considered the presence of monuments and other architectural works of importance, archaeological sites, folk art, and religious traditions.

---

### The Top Ten Most Culturally Rich Countries of the World, According to UNESCO are:

| | |
|---|---|
| 1. China | 6. Germany |
| 2. Spain | 7. Japan |
| 3. Italy | 8. India |
| 4. France | 9. United Kingdom |
| 5. Mexico | 10. Iran[153] |

⚜ France has the fourth-highest number of UNESCO World Heritage sites in the world (thirty-nine), tying with Germany. Italy tops the list (fifty), followed by China (forty-seven) and Spain (forty-four).[154]

## The Complete List of UNESCO World Heritage Sites in France is as Follows:

Abbey Church of Saint-Savin sur Gartempe

Cistercian Abbey of Fontenay

Arles, Roman and Romanesque Monuments

Vézelay, Church and Hill

Nord-Pas de Calais Mining Basin

Belfries of Belgium and France

Bordeaux, Port of the Moon

Canal du Midi

Amiens Cathedral

Bourges Cathedral

Chartres Cathedral

Cathedral of Notre-Dame, Former Abbey of Saint-Remi, and Palace of Tau, Reims

Historical Center of Avignon: Papal Palace, Episcopal Ensemble, and Avignon Bridge

Routes of Santiago de Compostela in France

Episcopal City of Albi

From the Great Saltworks of Salins-les-Bains to the Royal Saltworks of Arc-et-Senans, the Production of Open-pan Salt

Fortifications of Vauban

Decorated Cave of Pont d'Arc, Known as Grotte Chauvet–Pont d'Arc, Ardèche

Jurisdiction of Saint-Émilion

Le Havre, the City Rebuilt
by Auguste Perret

The Causses and the
Cévennes, Mediterranean
Agro-Pastoral Cultural
Landscape

Mont-Saint-Michel and
Its Bay

Palace and Park of
Fontainebleau

Palace and Park of
Versailles

Paris, Banks of the
Seine

Place Stanislas, Place de la
Carrière, and Place
d'Alliance in Nancy

Pont du Gard

Provins, Town of Medieval
Fairs

Historic site of Lyon

Prehistoric Pile Dwellings
around the Alps

Prehistoric Sites and
Decorated Caves of the
Vézère Valley

Strasbourg—Grande Île

Roman Theater and Its
Surroundings and the
"Triumphal Arch" of
Orange

The Loire Valley between
Sully-sur-Loire and
Chalonnes

Historic Fortified City of
Carcassonne

Gulf of Porto: Calanche of
Piana, Gulf of Girolata,
Scandola Reserve

Lagoons of New Caledonia:
Reef Diversity and
Associated Ecosystems

The Pitons, Cirques, and
Remparts of Réunion
Island

Pyrénées—Mont Perdu[155]

꧁ On a less picturesque note, over half the world's traffic roundabouts are to be found in France, which, with more than thirty thousand roundabouts, has more *ronds points* than any country in the world.[156]

꧄ The most visited attraction in France (and indeed, in the whole of Europe) is not the Eiffel Tower or the Louvre, but Disneyland Paris, with 14.2 million visits in 2014.[157]

꧄ The French national anthem, "*La Marseillaise*," was composed not in Marseilles but in Strasbourg, by French army officer Claude-Joseph Rouget de Lisle. The original title of the song was "War Song of the Army of the Rhine." It was adopted as the country's National Anthem in 1795. It acquired its nickname, "*La Marseillaise*," from its being sung by troops from Marseilles marching on the capital.[158]

꧄ The world's most expensive hotel is in France. The hotel Martinez in Cannes charges $37,200 a night for its penthouse suite.[159]

꧄ The most common surname in France is Martin. The top ten French surnames, with numbers of people bearing that name, are:

| | | |
|---|---|---|
| 1. | Martin | 236,172 |
| 2. | Bernard | 131,901 |
| 3. | Thomas | 119,078 |
| 4. | Dubois | 114,001 |
| 5. | Durand | 111,510 |
| 6. | Robert | 106,161 |
| 7. | Moreau | 103,056 |
| 8. | Petit | 95,876 |

| 9. | Simon | 95,733 |
| 10. | Michel | 93,581 |

*Classement des noms les plus portés, aufeminin.com*

♕ One in five French people suffers from depression, making France the most depressed country in the world.[160]

## ...Franglais

♕ *Franglais* is a derogatory French portmanteau made up of the words *français* ("French") and *anglais* ("English").* It is used to denote the wholesale importation of English words in French daily language usage—for example, *le weekend, le shopping*, etc. The term was first used by the French writer René Etiemble in his book *Parlez-vous franglais?* (1964), a diatribe against the incursion of English words into the French language.

**Common examples of *franglais* in everyday French:**
*Le weekend*
*Le marketing*
*Le shopping*
*Le baby boom*
*Le snack bar* (ironically, English usage would be the
 French word *buffet*)
*Le talkie-walkie* (walkie-talkie)

---

*Portmanteau: a word that combines two words to make a new one; for example, the English word *smog* (*smoke* + *fog*).

*Un look*

*Un parking* (parking lot)

*Un must* (ironically, English usage would be the French
    phrase *de rigueur*)

*Un chewing gum*

**Peculiar *franglais* words that appear to be based on
a misunderstanding of an English word:**

*Un relooking* (makeover)

*Le footing* (jogging)

*Un training* (track suit)

*Un egghead* (idiot)

*Un jerk* (excellent dancer)

*Un dressing* (walk-in wardrobe)

*Un smoking* (stylish jacket/smoking jacket)

Some of these mistranslations of English words can be
attributed to the phenomenon of *sesquilingualism*: that is, the
mastery of one-and-a-half languages (from the Latin *sesqui*,
meaning "one and a half"). The theory has it that when the half
language is perceived as cool or highly prestigious, it gets scat-
tered into the other language to make the speaker look sophis-
ticated and progressive, without a true understanding of the
original meaning of the words.[161]

👑 The Académie Française is a French institution dedicated
to the preservation of the French language—a job that has,
in recent years, included fighting *franglais*. The Académie
was founded by Cardinal Richelieu in 1635. Presided over by
forty dignitaries known as the *immortels* ("immortals"), its
principal role is to make rulings on the correct usage of the

French language. The Académie occupies a lavish building, the French Institute, on the banks of the River Seine. Each member has a numbered armchair, or *fauteuil,* for the whole of his life. The Académie periodically publishes new editions of a vast dictionary called *Dictionnaire de l'Académie française.* The current edition is the ninth, the first volume of which (*A—Enzyme*) appeared in 1992. The second volume (*Eocène—Mappemonde*) was published in 2000, and the third (*Maquereau—Quotité*) appeared in 2011. Throughout its history, the main battle of the Académie has been to counteract the incursion of English words into the French language by devising French substitutes—such as *courriel* for e-mail. Unfortunately, this is a losing battle, in particular in relation to technological terms. *Le hardware, le software, le spam, poker, liker,* etc., have all entered everyday French parlance, despite the attempt by the authorities to introduce snappy French equivalents like *informaticien bricoleur* for "geek," and *élément d'une image numérique* for "pixel."[162]

## ...Frogs

The origins of the term *Frogs* as applied to the French is shrouded in mystery. The first such reference seems—somewhat ironically—to have come from the French themselves. As early as the sixteenth century, the great French apothecary and seer Nostradamus referred to the French as *crapauds* ("toads"). The term *frogs* was widely used to refer to the Parisians when most of Paris was a bog, or *marais.* "*Qu'en disent les grenouilles?*" ("What will the frogs say about it?") was, in the 1700s, a common phrase at the court in Versailles. In England,

"Nic Frog" was traditionally the name for a Dutchman. The transference of the term to the French seems to have taken place in the eighteenth century during the Napoleonic Wars, and was reinforced by the Gallic fondness for frogs' legs as a delicacy.[163]

 Frogs' legs first cropped up as a food in France in the twelfth century, as a result of an ordinance by the medieval Catholic church that monks could not eat meat. The monks, rather cunningly, got frogs' legs defined as fish. Local peasants quickly followed suit, and a national dish was born.[164]

In his *Grand dictionnaire de cuisine* (1873), the writer Alexandre Dumas notes that a man from the Auvergne region named Simon was to be found making "a most considerable fortune with frogs, sent to him from his region, which he fattened and then sold to the very finest restaurants in Paris, where this foodstuff was very much in fashion." Only the green frogs with black legs are considered edible, and the legs are the only parts that are ever served.[165]

Traditionally, American and British people have held a deep horror and antipathy to even the idea of eating the parts of amphibious creatures. The English food writer Elizabeth David noted, in her book *French Provincial Cooking*, "It is odd that frogs' legs, which are such delicate little morsels that surely even the most fastidious could not object to them, should inspire such horror in England." However, David included only one recipe for frogs' legs in the book, on the basis that at that time in England, they were virtually impossible to find, outside the occasional canned variety.[166]

## Classic French Frogs' Legs Recipe

Take a dozen frogs' legs, coat in flour, and sauté in butter for 10 to 12 minutes, until cooked through. The addition of chopped parsley, garlic, and lemon juice will turn this into *cuisses de grenouille à la Provençale*.

To be drunk with the frogs' legs: dry white wine only, never red, which will drown the delicate flavor of the dish. Try Chablis, Côte de Beaune, or Pouilly-Fuissé.

Despite their avowed horror of frogs' legs, the British embraced them with enthusiasm for a brief period at the beginning of the last century, when the great chef Georges-Auguste Escoffier served them at a grand soirée in honor of the Prince of Wales at London's Savoy Hotel in 1908. The frogs' legs were cooked in a court bouillon with aromatic herbs, cooled, doused with a paprika sauce, then decorated with tarragon leaves and covered with chicken jelly. Escoffier cunningly called his creation *Cuisses de Nymphe à l'Aurore* ("Thighs of the Dawn Nymphs"). Nymphs' Thighs became the culinary hit of the season, possibly because most Edwardians did not realize they were consuming not the heavenly limbs of a lesser deity of classical mythology, but imported French bullfrogs.*[167]

---

*Euphemisms have commonly been used when attempting to introduce exotic foodstuffs to the conservative Anglo-American palate. Thus, when horsemeat was introduced into England in the mid-nineteenth century, it was referred to as *chevaline delicacies*.

The consumption of frogs' legs has declined massively in France in recent years, partly due to the hunting of native frog species to virtual extinction. They are now largely associated with retro cuisine from the regions, or Asian cooking, in which they are still widely used. However, Parisian restaurants often keep them on the menu as a curiosity for tourists. The world's biggest importer of frogs' legs today is not France, but the United States, which imported an impressive 21,491 tons in the course of the last decade.[168]

# G Is for...

## ...Garlic

☙ There are over twenty-five varieties of garlic grown in France. They can be divided broadly into two categories: fall/autumn garlic (*l'ail d'automne*), which is white or purple in color, and spring garlic (*l'ail de printemps*), which is pink in color.

The varieties of French garlic are named after the months in the Republican Calendar, a short-lived and disastrous experiment in timekeeping introduced by the French government shortly after the Revolution of 1789. The government wished to remove all vestiges of religion from the calendar, so traditional Saints' Days were replaced with alternatives intended to evoke French rural life, such as the Day of Celery and the Turnip. The varieties of French garlic therefore include Germidour (from "Germinal," the first month of spring), Messidrome (from "Messidor," the first month of summer), and Fructidor (the final summer month).[169]

[See further: entry for Republican Calendar under *Revolution*]

☙ Alexandre Dumas, in his *Grand dictionnaire de cuisine*, observed that "everybody recognizes the smell of garlic, except the person who has eaten it, and cannot therefore understand why all turn away at his approach." He also noted that the cuisine of Provence was particularly "based on garlic," and that the very air of Provence was "impregnated with the perfume of this herb."

✤ The French word for a sweater, *chandail*, is an abbreviation of *marchand d'ail*, a reference to the sellers of garlic in the traditional Parisian markets, who used to wear heavy-knit sweaters.[170]

✤ Consumption of garlic in France has gone down massively in recent years, as the French move away from local and regional cuisine to embrace a wider range of lighter and more international foods. The world's biggest consumers of garlic today are not in fact the French but the Koreans, who eat a massive 22 pounds of garlic per capita annually. Nor are the French in the top rank of garlic producers. World garlic production is headed by China, which produces 75 percent of the world's garlic.[171]

## ...Galette des rois

✤ The *galette des rois* ("kings' cake") is an ancient French tradition related to the Epiphany. On or around the sixth of January, families share a pastry cake or *galette*, in which is hidden a small porcelain charm or *fève* ("bean"). The cake comes accompanied by a paper crown, and the person who gets the slice of *galette* that contains the *fève* is crowned king for the day. The traditional accompaniment to the *galette* is apple cider.

Louis XIV was said to be particularly partial to the tradition of the *galette des rois*. In his day, the cake was divided into parts equal to the number of guests, with an extra part dedicated to the Virgin Mary, to be distributed to the poor (a tradition that continues in certain parts of France).[172]

♕ During the French Revolution, the future of the *galette des rois* came under serious threat. There was talk of banning a cake so intimately connected with the monarchy and established religion. Ultimately, the controversial cake was rechristened *la galette d'égalité* ("equality cake"), with no *fève*, and without the offensive appellation of *roi*. Today, the cake has reverted back to its original regal name in the *boulangeries* of France, and contains a *fève* once more. However, each year, the artisan *boulangers* of Paris present to the president's residence, the Élysée Palace, a special *galette* containing no *fève*. This *galette de l'Elysée* is an enduring reminder that no French president can ever be crowned king.[173]

♕ People who collect the *fèves*, or porcelain charms found hidden inside the *galettes de roi*, are called *fabophiles*.

♕ Some years ago, an astute Parisian *boulanger* hit upon the idea of concealing a *fève* of solid gold in one of his *galettes des rois*. He did more business in one morning than in a typical month. The idea caught on, and enterprising French bakers have since started concealing diamonds, gold coins, precious stone rings, and even money-back vouchers inside their Epiphany cakes. Although—to avoid the risk of a customer swallowing a $2,000 diamond—a plastic token is usually inserted into the winning cake, exchangeable on presentation for the prize.

## ...Guillotine

♕ The guillotine—the notorious instrument of execution during the French Revolution—owes its name, ironically, to a vociferous opponent of capital punishment. Joseph-Ignace Guillotin (1738–1814) was a French doctor who was shocked at the beheadings and violent executions of the French Revolution, and proposed that a more humane alternative be created. Early versions of the guillotine had already been used in Scotland. Under Dr. Guillotin's overall supervision, plans for a new and modified form were prepared. A German harpsichord maker named Tobias Schmidt built the first prototype, which, after being successfully tried out on some hospital corpses, was put into use by the French government. Dr. Guillotin was horrified when his name was given to the instrument that he had originally conceived, and which had—thanks to the years of the Terror—become associated with extreme bloodthirstiness and violence. After Guillotin's death, his family changed their name to dissociate themselves from the dreaded instrument.[174]

⚜ The first man to be executed by guillotine in France was a highwayman called Nicolas-Jacques Pelletier in 1792.[175]

⚜ The last public guillotining in France took place at Versailles in 1939. The guillotine was used for the final time in 1977, for the execution of the convicted Tunisian murderer Hamida Djandoubi. He was also the last person to be executed in France.[176]

⚜ During the 1790s, two-foot-tall miniature guillotine replicas were a popular toy in France. Children used these fully operational guillotines to decapitate dolls, or even small rodents. These charming toys were eventually banned by some communes, out of fear that they would make children ferocious and bloodthirsty. Novelty guillotines also found their way onto the dinner tables of the wealthy, where they were used as bread and vegetable slicers.[177]

⚜ At and after the time of the French Revolution, "victims' balls" became all the rage among a certain louche category of aristocrats with a black sense of humor. Only persons who had lost a member of the family to the guillotine were invited to the ball. Guests wore a red ribbon around their neck to symbolize the guillotine blade, and revelers performed a special dance, which involved a sudden jerk of the head to imitate the action of beheading. These morbid parties became hugely popular, with some people even falsely claiming to have had relatives who had been guillotined in order to get a chance of an invitation.[178]

⚜ The leading executioners in France from the time of the Revolution onward became cult heroes. The job was frequently passed on from father to son, with certain families dominating the profession—the Sanson family, for example, who guillotined King Louis XVI and Marie-Antoinette, and the Deiblers, who dominated in the late nineteenth and early twentieth centuries. People would chant their name in the streets, and the clothes they wore on the scaffold would often inspire fashion trends. Criminals, also, had a grim fascination for the leading executioners: it was not uncommon, for example, for gangsters and other members of the underworld to sport tattoos with inscriptions such as *"My head goes to Deibler."*[179]

# H Is for...

## ...Hashish

♛ The French are the second-largest consumers of cannabis in Europe, after the Czechs.[180]

Hashish was introduced to France indirectly by Napoleon, as a result of the French invasion of Egypt in 1798. French soldiers were used to whiling away their cares with alcohol, but in Muslim Egypt, alcohol was not the drug of choice. Instead, the preferred mind-bender was hashish. Napoleon's men took to the Arab habit with enthusiasm, so much so that in October 1800, Napoleon issued the following order to the French army of occupation:

> It is forbidden in all of Egypt to use certain Muslim beverages made with hashish or likewise to inhale the smoke from seeds of hashish. Habitual drinkers and smokers of this plant lose their reason and are victims of violent delirium, which is the lot of those who give themselves full to excesses of all sorts.

The edict had little effect. Napoleon had brought three scientists with him to study the country and its people: An-

toine Isaac Silvestre de Sacy, Pierre-Charles Rouyer, and
René-Nicolas Desgenettes. They also began using hashish,
ostensibly to see for themselves what this drug did to the
human body. Intrigued by their experiences, they sent some
back to France for their colleagues to conduct further experi-
ments in their laboratories. The first of these studies to be published appeared in 1803 by a Dr. Virey, who made various
extracts of hashish, hoping to track down the drug's elusive
active principle. After studying the drug at length, it was
Virey's opinion that hashish was nothing less than the mysterious potion nepenthe, said to have been used by Helen of
Troy to drug her guests into a stupor of forgetfulness.[181]

On his return from the Napoleonic wars in Egypt, Antoine Isaac Silvestre de Sacy, one of the trio sent by Napoleon
and a leading Arabic scholar of the time, announced that he
had found the key to the origins of the name of the Assassins—
the Arab cutthroats who had terrorized the Middle East
at the time of the Crusades. The word *assassin*, de Sacy said,
originated from the word *hashish* (Arabic *ḥašīši*). The Arabic
word was probably originally a derogatory nickname, with
reference to the supposedly erratic behavior of the members
of the sect, as if intoxicated by hashish. Other suggestions
were that the Assassins were so called because they were actually addicted to hashish; or alternatively, because they were
encouraged by their leader to consume hashish before a mission to assassinate Christian adversaries, so that, from the resulting hallucinatory visions, they might gain a foretaste of
the joys of paradise that awaited them on completion of their
mission.[182]

꩜ The French poet Charles Baudelaire wrote extensively on the subject of hashish, including his lengthy "Poem of Hashish," in which he described the sensation of cannabis smoking in these terms:

> There! there is happiness; heaven in a teaspoon; happiness, with all its intoxication, all its folly, all its childishness. You can swallow it without fear; it is not fatal; it will in nowise injure your physical organs. Perhaps (later on) too frequent an employment of the sorcery will diminish the strength of your will; perhaps you will be less a man than you are today; but retribution is so far off, and the nature of the eventual disaster so difficult to define! What is it that you risk? A little nervous fatigue to-morrow—no more.[183]

꩜ One of the most notorious recipes ever published is that for hashish fudge, devised by Alice B. Toklas (1877–1967). A member of the "lost generation" of expat writers living in Paris in the inter-war years, Toklas was the partner of the famous modernist author Gertrude Stein. Their home in Paris—27 rue de Fleurus, in the 6th arrondissement—became notorious as a salon where the likes of Pablo Picasso, Ernest Hemingway, F. Scott Fitzgerald, and Henri Matisse would meet to discuss ideas and partake of rather unconventional foodstuffs. An enthusiastic cook, Alice published her memoirs in 1954 as *The Alice B. Toklas Cook Book*, which included a recipe for hashish fudge. This caused an uproar on publication. The recipe was expunged from the American version of the cookbook, but left in the British. Toklas described her hashish fudge as "the food

## Alice B. Toklas's Recipe for Hashish Fudge

Take 1 teaspoon black peppercorns, 1 whole nutmeg,
4 average sticks of cinnamon, 1 teaspoon coriander.
These should all be pulverized in a mortar. About a
handful each of de-stoned dates, dried figs, shelled
almonds and peanuts: chop these and mix them together.
A bunch of cannabis *sativa* can be pulverized. This
along with the spices should be dusted over the mixed
fruit and nuts, kneaded together. About a cup of sugar
dissolved in a big pat of butter. Rolled into a cake and
cut into pieces or made into balls about the size of a
walnut, it should be eaten with care. Two pieces are
quite sufficient.

Obtaining the cannabis may present certain diffi-
culties, but the variety known as cannabis *sativa* grows
as a common weed, often unrecognized, everywhere
in Europe, Asia and parts of Africa; besides being
cultivated as a crop for the manufacture of rope. In
the Americas, while often discouraged, its cousin,
called cannabis *indica*, has been observed even in
city window boxes. It should be picked and dried as
soon as it has gone to seed and while the plant is
still green.

*The Alice B. Toklas Cook Book*
by Alice B. Toklas[185]

of Paradise—of Baudelaire's artificial paradises." It might, she said, provide "entertaining refreshment for a Ladies Bridge Club or a chapter meeting of the DAR (Daughters of the American Revolution)." Toklas warned, however, that consumption could produce interesting effects: "Euphoria and brilliant storms of laughter; ecstatic reveries and extensions of one's personality on several simultaneous planes are to be complacently expected. Almost anything Saint Theresa did, you can do better if you can bear to be ravished by *un évanouissement reveillé*."[184]

# I Is for...

## ...Invention

♛ Many of the world's most groundbreaking inventions were by Frenchmen, some of whose names have entered the English language. Gallic eponyms—that is, English-language words named after the French people who invented or otherwise inspired the ideas or concepts behind them—include:[186]

- *Braille.* The Braille system of reading and writing for the blind was invented in 1824 by a Frenchman, Louis Braille (1809–1852), who lost his eyesight as a child. Braille developed a system of rectangular blocks containing raised dots. The arrangement of the dots distinguished one character from another.
- *Diesel.* A French-born German engineer, Rudolf Diesel (1858–1913) is credited with inventing the diesel engine. He patented the design for a new, more efficient internal combustion engine in 1892. The first prototype was exhibited in 1897.
- *Praline.* The chocolatier's term for an almond coated in cooked sugar was created in the seventeenth century by Clément Jaluzot, the personal chef of the Comte de Plessis-Praslin (1598–1675), a sugar industrialist and

military man. Legend has it that the Comte asked his chef to produce a special treat to tantalize the ladies, with the result that the first *praslines* were created, exquisitely packaged in small boxes.

- *Magnolia.* The heavily perfumed, off-white blooms were discovered in 1703 on the island of Martinique and are named after Pierre Magnol (1638–1715), an influential French botanist who first proposed that plants should be grouped in "families" according to shared characteristics. Similarly, the brilliant red and purple tropical flowers known as bougainvillea are named after the eighteenth-century French explorer Louis-Antoine de Bougainville (1729–1811).

- *Pasteurization.* The technique of heating milk to a high temperature, followed by immediate cooling, to kill off germs, is named after the Frenchman Louis Pasteur (1822–1895), who invented it. Originally, pasteurization was used for preserving wines and beer, but its extension to the preservation of milk in the late nineteenth century is believed to have saved millions of lives since.

- *Leotard.* The one-piece outfit used in dance and gymnastics is named after a Frenchman, Jules Léotard (1842–1870). Léotard was an acrobat who virtually invented the flying trapeze in the 1850s, by experimenting with ropes and bars over his home swimming pool in Toulouse. He would perform in a tight-fitting garment of his own design, which he called the *mail-*

*lot.* After his tragic and early death at the age of twenty-eight, however, people started to refer to it as the *leotard.*

- *Silhouette.* The word comes from Étienne de Silhouette (1709–1767), a particularly unpopular eighteenth-century French finance minister who introduced draconian austerity measures during the Seven Years' War between England and France. The term *silhouette* was used with black humor to describe the simple black profiles that the rich were reduced to commissioning as a result of his cutbacks, replacing the lavish oil portraits of previous decades.

- *Chauvinism.* Defined as: 1. Militant devotion to and glorification of one's country; fanatical patriotism. 2. Prejudiced belief in the superiority of one's own gender, group, or kind. The term comes from a (probably fictitious) legendary French soldier called Nicolas Chauvin, who is supposed to have served in Napoleon's army, and is credited with dozens of supremely patriotic acts. Since nobody has found an official record of Nicolas Chauvin, he probably never existed.

- *Sadism.* Defined as: Enthusiasm for inflicting pain, suffering, or humiliation on others; especially, a psychological disorder characterized by sexual fantasies, urges, or behavior involving the subjection of another person to pain. Named after the infamous Comte Donatien-Alphonse-François, Marquis de Sade (1740–1814), notorious French libertine and author of the erotic novel *Les 120 Journées de Sodome* (*One Hundred and Twenty Days of Sodom*).*

- *Clementine.* This "accidental" hybrid between a mandarin and a regular orange was discovered in 1902 and cultivated in the arid hills of Algeria by Marie-Clément Rodier (1839–1904), a French missionary who ran an orphanage there.
- *Bic biro*, used to refer to a ballpoint pen. A ballpoint pen developed in 1949 by the Frenchman Marcel Bich (1914–1994) from prototypes he had seen in Argentina, manufactured by Laszlo Biro. The Bich company in Hauts-de-Seine, France, still manufactures the Bic Cristal, which is the best-selling pen in the world (the 100 billionth Bic pen was sold in September 2006).†

⚜ The French word for trash can—*poubelle*—is in fact an eponym and derives from a certain Monsieur Poubelle, who—put out by the stink of Paris in the 1880s—introduced a few hygiene measures. As Prefect of Paris, Poubelle decreed in 1884 that owners of buildings had to provide the people who lived there with covered containers, to hold household refuse. Soon dubbed *boîtes Poubelle* by the press, the name stuck.[187]

---

*The inverse of sadism—masochism—comes from Leopold von Sacher-Masoch (1836–1895), an Austrian novelist who, like the Marquis de Sade, wrote about his sexual fantasies and experiences. In Masoch's case he wrote about how he agreed to be the slave of his mistress, Baroness Fanny Pistor, for six months, as long as she wore furs while humiliating him.

†For the name change of Bich to Bic, see the entry for *Bich* under the subject title *Misnomers & Misunderstandings*.

[See also: *Nicotine*, under subject title *Cigarette*; also, subject title *Guillotine*.]

## ...Isadora Duncan

The American dancer Isadora Duncan (1877–1927) was one of the highest-paid performers of the early twentieth century. Famously renamed by the American writer Dorothy Parker as "Duncan Disorderly," Duncan made her home in France and died tragically there. Born to a poor family in San Francisco, Isadora took the world by storm when she rejected the moves of conventional ballet, reinterpreting dance as a free and natural movement, and dancing barefoot in a Greek tunic. A fierce opponent of marriage, Duncan had numerous affairs and a string of children by different fathers, two of whom died as infants when the family's chauffeur-driven Bentley crashed into the River Seine. In 1922, against her long-held beliefs, Duncan married the Russian poet Sergei Yesenin, mainly to help him get out of Russia. The marriage was a stormy one, ending when the poet slashed his wrists and wrote a final elegy in his own blood. Isadora herself finally settled down to a somewhat seedy existence in the French Riviera town of Nice. One day, she took a spin on the famous Nice esplanade, the Promenade des Anglais, in a borrowed Bugatti. The fringes of her long red scarf were blown back in the wind and caught on the rear-wheel spokes. Duncan was almost hurled out of the car. She was killed instantly, virtually decapitated by her scarf. The incident led the American expat author Gertrude Stein to make the mordant remark that "affectations can be dangerous."

An unwitting legacy of Duncan's was to give the medical profession a name for the injury known as "Isadora Duncan Syndrome," which results when an article of clothing or hair becomes entangled in a piece of machinery or moving object.*

---

*This injury is apparently common in India, where flowing garments such as saris frequently become entangled in the wheels of rickshaws. It has also been seen in Europe, at cultural events such as the Edinburgh Festival in Scotland, where cycle-propelled rickshaws are popular as alternatives to taxis.[188]

# J Is for...

## ...Joke

♔ April Fools' Day, on the first of April—a day informally dedicated to practical jokes, hoaxes, and pranks—is believed to have originated in France, although the precise nature of how it arose remains shrouded in mystery. One prominent theory is that the custom started in the late 1500s, when France moved to the Gregorian calendar. As a result of the change, January 1 became New Year's Day, instead of March 25 (the day of the Annunciation, or the revelation of the Angel Gabriel to the Virgin Mary that she was to be the mother of the future Messiah), as it had been previously. Those country bumpkins ignorant of this fact still celebrated the New Year in the week of March 25 to April 1, leading to this day being dedicated to fools.[189]

The French call April Fools' Day *poisson d'avril* ("April Fish Day"). It is celebrated by pinning a paper fish on an unsuspecting person's back. This is a particularly popular tradition with French schoolchildren, generally tolerated by teachers, with the result that it is a common sight to see the backs of normally rather severe French primary teachers festooned with paper stickers on April 1. There are a number of explanations as to how the tradition of *poisson d'avril* started. They include the theory that it originates from Pisces being the last winter sign of the Zodiac, from whose house the sun moves in the month of April; or that it simply refers to the gullibility of fish that take the bait.[190]

As in other countries, the French media delight in fooling their readers with silly stories designed to trap the gullible on April Fish Day. Famous examples of Gallic April Fish Day hoaxes include:

- 1972: The radio station France Inter announced that, following the forthcoming accession of Britain to the European Union (1973), cars would be driven on the left side of roads, to help British motorists in France. Almost immediately, the radio station's lines were jammed with phone calls from enraged French motorists.[191]
- 1986: The French newspaper *Le Parisien* reported that an agreement had been signed for the Eiffel Tower to be dismantled and reconstructed in the Euro Disney theme park.[192]
- 2006: French television presenter and food critic Jean-Pierre Coffe announced on a food program that a new variety of blue wine was to be introduced.[193]
- 2013: The French MP Jean-Frédéric Poisson announced that a law was to be introduced to protect French politicians with "aquatic animal surnames" from being ridiculed on April Fish Day. Backers of the proposal were said to include the politicians Franck Marlin and Philippe Goujon. The MP Jean-Marie Tétart objected to the proposal, even though his name

sounds the same as the word for "tadpole" in French (*un têtard*).[194]

- 2014: France Inter announced on its news that, because of budgetary cuts, the mayor of Paris had decided to sell the Eiffel Tower to the Arab state of Qatar.[195]

## ...Jewels

♛ One of the most famous jewels of all time is the French Blue. This was a diamond obtained by Louis XIV from the French explorer Jean-Baptiste Tavernier (1605–1689), who brought it from India in 1671. The diamond was noted for its rare blue hue and its unusual attribute of emitting a dull red glow when exposed to sunlight, which earned it the reputation of bringing ill luck to those who wore it. The French jeweler Jean Pittan cut it to lustrous perfection over two years, and the diamond was set in a brooch that Louis XIV had pinned to his cravat for special occasions. Later, it was worn by Louis XV in a more splendid setting, as a pendant for the Order of the Golden Fleece. The diamond disappeared in the turmoil and general ransacking of royal treasures that occurred during the French Revolution. Twenty years later, however, a mysterious blue diamond matching its description appeared at a London jeweler, from which it entered the collection of the Dutch/London banker Henry Phillip Hope. Hope rechristened the gem after himself, as the "Hope Diamond." The diamond was bought in 1910 by Pierre Cartier and subsequently sold to the American jeweler Harry Winston, who donated it in 1958 to the Smithsonian Institute in Washington. Unsubstantiated rumors that the celebrated Hope Diamond was in fact the French Blue, recut, persisted until 2007, when a lead model of the French Blue was discovered in the archives of the French natural history museum. The fit was perfect and proved, beyond a doubt, that the Hope was a recut of a larger piece taken from the original French Blue. The mythical Hope Diamond/ French Blue remains at the Smithsonian, and is its most prized exhibit. Rumored to be insured for $250 million, it is the second most-visited museum object in the world, after the *Mona Lisa*.[196]

The French Blue has long had a reputation for bringing bad luck to those who own it. This is partly because of the dull red glow that the diamond emits when exposed to sunlight, and partly due to the legend that the French explorer Tavernier, who originally discovered it, removed it from its original setting in an Indian temple, as the eye of a Hindu idol. In 1911, *The New York Times* published a colorful account of the fates of the gem's alleged various owners (although experts have questioned the veracity of some of these attributions):

- Jacques Colet bought the Hope Diamond from Simon Frankel, and committed suicide.
- Prince Ivan Kanitovski bought the diamond from Colet, but was killed by Russian revolutionists.
- Kanitovski loaned the diamond to Madame Ladue, who was "murdered by her sweetheart."
- Simon Mencharides, who had once sold it to the Turkish sultan, was thrown from a precipice along with his wife and young child.
- Sultan Hamid gave it to Abu Sabir to "polish," but later Sabir was imprisoned and tortured.

- Stone guardian Kulub Bey was hanged by a mob in Turkey.
- A Turkish attendant named Hehver Agha was hanged for having it in his possession.
- Tavernier, who brought the stone from India to Paris, was "torn to pieces by wild dogs in Constantinople."
- King Louis gave it to Madame de Montespan, whom he later abandoned.
- Nicolas Fouquet, an "Intendant of France," borrowed it temporarily to wear it, but was "disgraced and died in prison."
- A temporary wearer, Princess de Lamballe, was "torn to pieces by a French mob."
- Jeweler William Fals, who recut the stone, "died a ruined man."
- William Fals's son Hendrik stole the jewel from his father and later "committed suicide."
- Some years after Hendrik's theft of the jewel, the diamond was "sold to Francis Deaulieu, who died in misery and want."[197]

The biggest diamond heist in history occurred in Cannes, France, in 2013. On July 28, a man entered the Carlton International Hotel in Cannes. His target was jewelry worth $116 million. He pulled off the theft in just one and a half minutes. The diamonds belonged to the Soviet diamond mogul Lev Leviev, and had been on display at an exhibition in the hotel.[198]

The world's most valuable Easter egg is an Imperial Fabergé egg, made by the French house of Fabergé and estimated to be worth over $30 million. And yet, its location remains a mystery. The Imperial Fabergé eggs were a series of magnificent Easter eggs created by the Franco-Russian House of Fabergé for the Russian royal family between 1885 and 1916. Only fifty Imperial Eggs were made. The locations of forty-three of them are known. Six are believed to have been lost, melted down for scrap. However, one remaining egg—known as the *Nécessaire* ("Necessary")—was purchased by an anonymous buyer from a jewelry shop in Bond Street, London, in 1952. Only one photograph exists of the egg sold to the stranger, which is made from gold in the Louis XV style, set with precious stones. Perhaps it may yet resurface one day, like the forty-third known Fabergé Imperial egg, which was discovered in 2014 by a scrap dealer in the American Midwest and purchased for a mere $13,000.[199]

# K Is for...

## ...King

♔ *Dauphin*, the title traditionally held by the eldest son of the king of France, literally means "dolphin." The title was originally attached to certain French landed estates, and passed to the eldest son of the king of France in the fourteenth century.[200]

♔ King Charles VI of France (1368–1422), suffered under the delusion that he was made of glass. He even had iron bars sewn into his clothes, to protect him from shattering if he fell. As a young ruler Charles had appeared reasonably normal, and was known as the "Much Beloved." After a "febrile illness," however, he became known as Charles le Fou ("Charles the Mad"). He once tore down the palace  halls howling like a wolf, and even shot members of his own entourage in a fit of insanity. Cutting holes in his scalp was considered, after application of a liquid made from powdered pearls failed to cure him. Exorcism also failed to do the trick; the tortured king merely pleaded with the caster of the spell to let him die.[201]

♔ Diane de Poitiers (1499–1566) was the mistress of King

Henri II, of whom she was senior by twenty years. Henri II made her a duchess and gave her the exquisite Loire château of Chenonceau. Diane's beauty was as renowned at the age of sixty as it had been at fifteen, when she was married off to her husband, Louis de Brézé. The source of her eternal beauty remained a mystery: some whispered about the influence of sorcery. Diane's beauty secrets, however, seem on the whole sensibly modern, and can be summarized as follows:

---

### Beauty Secrets of Diane de Poitiers

---

- Summer and winter, in all weathers, she would rise at dawn and bathe her whole body in ice-cold rain or well water.

- She breakfasted simply, with a cup of homemade broth or bouillon, then went for a brisk three-hour horse ride in the countryside around Chenonceau.

- She had a great penchant for lotions and potions, and prepared face masks, one of which was a famous concoction of melon juice, crushed young barley, and egg yolk mixed with ambergris (a type of sperm whale vomit).

- She favored sleeping (that is, when alone and not with the king) in a semi-upright position, propped up on pillows, to slow the forces of gravity and stop creases to the face.[202]

---

☜ Charles V, Holy Roman Emperor (1500–1558), was one of the most powerful rulers of the sixteenth century, with an empire that extended over Germany, Austria, parts of the

Lowlands, and modern-day France, including the Duchy of Burgundy. He had, however, some curious peccadilloes. Perhaps the strangest was his determination to mastermind his own death arrangements. This was so much so, that he presided over rehearsals of his own funeral many times. He had his servants file into the church in a procession, holding black candles. He himself followed them, wrapped in a shroud. Once in the church, Charles lay down in the coffin he had preselected and joined in the prayers for his soul.[203]

⚜ Charles IX (1550–1574) was one of France's most eccentric monarchs. He suffered from melancholy, hysteria, and morbid hallucinations, made considerably worse after his role in the Saint Bartholomew's Day Massacre (August 24, 1572), a bloodbath in which up to ten thousand Huguenots (Protestant dissenters) were killed by the Paris mob over a period of five days. The king was consumed by terrible guilt for the killings, and claimed that he could hear the screams of murdered Huguenots ringing in his ears. He would alternately blame himself, crying: "What bloodshed! What murders! What evil counsel I have followed! O my God, forgive me . . . I am lost! I am lost!" Or he would blame his mother: "Who but you is the cause of all of this? God's blood, you are the cause of it all!" His mother, Catherine de' Medici, responded by declaring her son a lunatic. At the Palace of the Louvre, Charles was frequently to be seen charging down the corridors with a saddle on his back. Perhaps thankfully for all, he died at the Château de Vincennes at twenty-three years old.[204]

⚜ The European king with the longest rule in history was Louis XIV of France (1643–1715), the "Sun King." Louis ruled France for 72 years, 3 months, and 18 days. The second-longest-reigning monarch was Franz Joseph I (1848–1916), Emperor of Austria and King of Hungary (68 years). Third came Ferdinand III of Sicily (1759–1825; 65 years), followed by Elizabeth II of England (1952–). Elizabeth II recently beat the previous British record holder, her great-great-grandmother Queen Victoria, as the longest-reigning British monarch (63 years).[205]

꙲ The American state of Louisiana is named after Louis XIV. In 1682 the French explorer Réne-Robert Cavelier de La Salle traveled down the Mississippi River and planted a cross with the arms of Louis XIV when he reached the Gulf of Mexico, claiming the whole area for France. He named the area Louisiane.[206]

꙲ Louis XIV was a legendary gourmand, capable of putting away vast quantities of food in a single sitting. Lunch (rather misnamed as *le petit couvert*) would typically consist of four different bowls of soup, a whole stuffed pheasant, a partridge, chicken, duck, mutton, ham, boiled eggs, three enormous salads, and a plate of pastries, fruit, and jam. Dinner would consist of a further forty dishes. When Louis died in 1715, his stomach and intestines were discovered to be twice the size of a normal man's.[207]

꙲ Two of the positions most sought after by courtiers in the court of King Louis XIV were those of the *Chevalier Porte-Coton* ("Knight of the Toilet Paper"), in charge of wiping the royal nether regions after a visit to the privy, and the *Porte-Chaise*, in charge of disposing of the privy contents after they had been inspected by the royal doctors. These offices were hard to come by: there were only seven in 1693, and only five in 1712. They must have been kept busy, though: due to his copious appetite, the king would visit his *garde-robe* up to twelve times a day.[208]

⚜ The modern birthing table was actually invented for the benefit of King Louis XIV. Louis, like many proud fathers, wished to witness the birth of his (many) children. As the birthing stools upon which women squatted obscured his view, he invented the "viewing table" so he could obtain as graphic a view as possible. The king's enthusiasm for the new birthing position soon caught on—to the detriment of millions of women since.[209]

⚜ As well as holding the record for the longest reign (Louis XIV), France also has the distinction of producing the shortest reign of any monarch in Europe. Louis XIX (1775–1844) became king on the abdication of his father on August 2, 1830, and himself abdicated in favor of Henry V just twenty minutes later.[210]

## ...Kiss

⚜ Everybody knows that the French exchange kisses (known as *les bises*) on greeting each other. But how many kisses, on which cheek(s), and in what order? Unfortunately for bewildered foreigners, the answer is that kissing practices in France vary widely from region to region. In Paris, the standard form is one kiss on each cheek. However, elsewhere in France, as many as four kisses may be exchanged. The general principle is that the reserved and conservative Parisians tend to limit displays of affection to two kisses, one on each cheek, while more effusive country folk may go up to as many as four.

♛ One of the most recognizable images in the world is the 1950 photograph by Robert Doisneau titled *Kiss by the Town Hall* (*Le baiser de l'hôtel de ville*), which portrays two lovers engaged in a passionate embrace on a busy Paris street in front of the Hôtel de Ville. The image has, however, a less than romantic history. The couple portrayed in the photograph, Françoise Bornet and her boyfriend, Jacques Carteaud, were two theater students that Doisneau had spotted embracing in a Parisian café. Doisneau paid them 500 francs for posing for the shot. When the photograph became a worldwide phenomenon years later, a couple called Lavergne came forward claiming to be the pair in the picture and seeking their share of the profits. This forced Doisneau to admit that the picture had been staged. Françoise Bornet then came forward, and to prove she was the woman really in the photograph, showed a numbered print that Doisneau had given her as a gift after the shot was taken. Bornet herself claimed royalties on sales of the photograph. The French court threw out the Lavergne couple's spurious claims but also rejected Bornet's claim for royalties, as she was not, the court ruled, recognizable in the photograph. Bornet had, by this time, split up with her boyfriend. In 2005, Bornet sold her print of the photograph at auction for €155,000 ($175,000)—more than ten times the expected price.[211]

♛ A critical mistake made by Anglophone visitors to France is to not understand that the French word for kiss (*un baiser*) totally changes meaning when it becomes a verb (*baiser*, which does *not* mean "to kiss," but something a lot more personal—to f\*\*\*). If, therefore, you greet someone with the remark *je veux vous baiser*, you might not get the cordial reaction you were hoping for. The correct French verb to use in this context is *embrasser*.

# L Is for...

## ...Language

♕ French is the second most studied foreign language in Europe, after English.[212]

♕ French is a language of Switzerland, Canada, Ivory Coast, Luxembourg, Monaco, Congo, and Niger.[213]

♕ In the United States, French is the second language in Louisiana, Vermont, Maine, and New Hampshire. The name of Vermont is from the French *vert mont*, meaning "green mountain."*

♕ The world's second-largest French-speaking city—after Paris—is Kinshasa (capital of the Democratic Republic of Congo), before Montreal and Brussels.[214]

♕ At the time of the French Revolution, 75 percent of the French population did not speak French as their mother tongue. Parisian French was imposed as the national language by way of an enforced program through education throughout the nineteenth and early twentieth centuries.[215]

♕ Almost 30 percent of English words derive from the French language.[216]

♕ The international distress code "Mayday" comes from

---

*For the nomenclature of Louisiana, see under subject heading *King*.

the French *M'aidez,* meaning "Help me!" Under the rules of radio signaling code, the word should be repeated three times ("Mayday-Mayday-Mayday") by a vessel or aircraft in a life-threatening situation. The word as a distress code was coined in 1923 by Frederick Stanley Mockford, a senior radio officer at Croydon airport, near London. Mockford was asked to think of a distress call that would be understood by all pilots and ground staff, and as much of the traffic at that time was between Croydon and Le Bourget airport, he hit on the idea of using the word "Mayday." Mayday signals the third and highest level of alert, after the first two levels, also based on French terms:

- *Sécurité* (pronounced *saycuritay*)—opens a report of potential danger to all listeners (e.g., a large log is drifting in a narrow channel)
- *Pan-pan* (pronounced *pahn-pahn*)—from the French *en panne,* meaning a breakdown. Indicates a potentially life-threatening situation, and the desire to have the position monitored (the ship has run into the log and suffered hull damage, but is not at serious risk).
- *Mayday/M'aidez* (pronounced *mayday*)—indicates a life-threatening situation and requests immediate aid (the ship is holed by the log and is sinking)
- *Silence Mayday* (pronounced *seelonce mayday*)—said by the coast guard or other agency to order silence on the radio channel; *silence distress* (pronounced *seelonce distress*) is the order to clear the radio channel of all other than emergency communications; *silence fini* (pronounced *seelonce feenee*) ends the radio silence after the emergency is over.[217]

꧁ In ancient times there developed in French the phrase *fils de bast*, meaning "child of the saddle." This referred to a child born to an unmarried mother, whose father had been a traveling herder, shepherd, or muleteer. He likely used his saddle as a pillow, and afterward slung it back on his horse or mule as he rode away. The phrase gradually extended to become associated with all children born to unmarried mothers and (in most cases) transient fathers, and became modified into the English word *bastard*—that is, a child born of the saddle rather than the marriage bed.[218]

꧁ The name of the flower, *dandelion*, comes from the French *dent de lion* ("tooth of a lion"), referring to the shape of its petals. The French term for dandelion is the rather less poetic *pissenlit* ("piss-in-bed"—referring to the allegedly diuretic properties of the plant, or possibly the lurid color of the flower).[219]

꧁ The English word *mortgage* comes from the French words *mort* ("death") and *gage* ("pledge"), with the cheerful sense that it's something you pledge to pay until you are dead.[220]

꧁ The term *love*, used to denote a score of zero in the game of tennis, probably comes from French. While there have been several explanations posited for this curious use of the word, the prevailing one is that it is a corruption of the French word for egg, *l'oeuf*, which was used to denote the egg shape of the figure zero. English and American umpires, being unable to pronounce the word *l'oeuf* correctly, corrupted it to "love."[221]

꧁ *Jusqu'auboutism* is defined as the policy of doggedly seeing something through to the very end. *Jusq'au bout* is the French equivalent of "to the bitter end," and suggests something being taken through to its conclusion. It first appeared in English in 1918, when the British writer George Bernard Shaw wrote that "in Constantinople it will be a matter of fighting *jusqu'au bout*." The writer Aldous Huxley also referred to himself as a *jusqu'au boutist* with respect to the war in France.[222]

There is a village in France called Condom (Gers)—although no official link to the word *condom*, signifying "French letter," has been established. The origins of the English word *condom* remain a mystery. Some say that it derives from the Persian word *kondü*, an earthenware receptacle for seeds or grains. Others claim that it relates to a certain Dr. Condom, personal physician to Charles II, who supposedly invented the device in the seventeenth century. However, to date, the existence of such a personage has not been established.[223]

Whereas the traditional English typists' warm-up is "The quick brown fox jumped over the lazy dog," French typists can use the phrase *"Allez porter ce vieux whisky au juge blond qui fume un havane,"* as it contains every letter in the French alphabet. The phrase translates as, 'Take this old whiskey to the blond judge who is smoking a cigar.'

As English has an enormous vocabulary, there are many English words with no French equivalent. They are often words of a practical nature. They include: [224]

- peck (*donner un coup de bec*)
- shallow (*peu profond*)
- clockwise (*dans le sens des aiguilles d'une montre*)
- counterclockwise (*dans le sens inverse des aiguilles d'une montre*)*

---

*Of course, as George Bush is famously supposed to have observed, the French also have no word for *entrepreneur*.

☙ There are also many French words with no single-word equivalents in English. They are often words of a poetic nature. They include:

- *dépaysement* (n.): the sensation of being in a foreign country.
- *chômer* (v.): to be unemployed—but perhaps tellingly, the French turn this into an active verb as opposed to a passive state of being.
- *retrouvailles* (n.): a happy reunion after a long time spent apart.
- *sortable* (adj.): someone you can take out anywhere without being embarrassed.
- *empêchement* (n.): a sudden or last-minute change of plans. This is a good excuse to explain a failure to keep an appointment without having to be specific as to the reasons.
- *flâner* (v.): A very difficult term to translate. Defined in the nineteenth century by the literary crowd of Paris as the art of leisurely strolling the streets of Paris, without any particular goal or destination, simply for the pleasure of soaking up the beauty of the city.
- *serein* (n.): the fine, light rain that falls from a clear sky at sunset or in the early hours of the night; evening serenity.
- *dérive* (n.): literally, "drift"; a spontaneous journey where the traveler leaves his or her life behind for a time, to let the spirit of the landscape and architecture attract and move him/her (a word fashionable with French intellectuals since the 1970s).

👑 Some French phrases with no conceptual equivalent in English include:

- *esprit d'escalier*: literally, "staircase wit"—the predicament of thinking of the perfect retort too late. The Germans have a single word for this incredibly annoying but common feeling: *treppenwitz*.
- *mise en abyme*: literally, "standing between two mirrors"—used to express the idea of infinite regression. Commonly used to refer to post-modern literature.
- *la douleur exquise*: the heart-wrenching pain of unrequited love.
- *l'appel du vide*: literally, "call of the void"—a sudden and inexplicable urge to jump when on a high ledge or in a high place.
- *chanter en yaourt*: literally, "to sing in yogurt"—someone trying to sing in a foreign language and getting the words mixed up. Frequently applicable to the singing of English-language pop songs on French talent shows.
- *à l'ouest*: not "in the west," which would be *dans l'ouest*, but literally "to the west," used to describe someone who thinks outside the box.
- *seigneur-terrasse*: a person who spends many hours but little money in a café. There are many such people in the cafés of Paris and other French cities.
- *mon jardin privé*: literally, "my own private garden"—used to denote one's right to a private fantasy world that nobody can enter without permission, be it a penchant for Scrabble or for cavorting around naked in a dog collar.

❧ English slang expressions and their French equivalents include:

English—When pigs fly

French—*Quand les poules auront des dents* ("When hens have teeth")

English—I have other fish to fry

French—*J'ai d'autres chats à fouetter* ("I have other cats to whip")

English—He has bats in the belfry

French—*Il a une araignée au plafond* ("He has a spider on the ceiling")

English—Don't count your chickens before they hatch

French - *Ne pas vendre la peau de l'ours avant de l'avoir tué* ("Don't sell the skin of the bear before having killed it")

## ...Literature

❧ France has won the most Nobel Prizes for Literature in the world. As of 2015, seventeen Nobel prizes for literature had been awarded to France.[225]

❧ The oldest surviving works of French literature are heroic poems dating from the twelfth century, known as the *chansons de geste*. The most famous of these is France's national epic, *La Chanson de Roland* (*The Song of Roland*). This tells the story of the Battle of Roncevaux in AD 778, during the reign of Charlemagne, and the exploits of the hero Roland. The oldest extant manuscript is held by Oxford's Bodleian Library.[226]

❧ The bestselling French book of all time is Antoine de Saint-Exupéry's whimsical children's story *Le Petit Prince* (1943), estimated to have sold over 80 million copies. It is the only French book to make the top twenty-five world sellers of all time.[227]

♛ The top selling author of all time in France is the British crime writer Agatha Christie, who beats Émile Zola into second place. The Queen of Crime is actually the most-read author of all time worldwide, with 2 billion copies of her books sold in 73 languages across 153 countries.[228]

♛ In 1863, the French writer Jules Verne wrote *Paris in the Twentieth Century*, a futuristic vision of Paris in the 1960s. The predictions Verne made were breathtakingly accurate: he foresaw the rise of feminism, mass suburban development, glass skyscrapers, and even the advent of e-mail and burglar alarms. However, Verne's publisher, Pierre-Jules Hetzel, rejected the story as simply unbelievable, so Verne locked it away in a safe where it was discovered by his great-grandson in 1989. It was finally published in Paris in 1994, and an English translation was published in 1996.[229]

♛ The model for the secret agent James Bond is said to have been a man named Wilfred "Biffy" Dunderdale, who was MI6's "man in Paris" during and after the Second World War. Biffy, so named because of his prowess as a boxer, is known to have been a friend of Ian Fleming, the author of the original James Bond books. He was described as "a man of great charm and savoir faire" with a "penchant for pretty women and fast cars."[230]

♛ "Sleeping Beauty," "Puss in Boots," "Little Red Riding Hood," "Tom Thumb," and "Cinderella" were fairy tales written by the French writer Charles Perrault (1628–1703). They were published under the title *Tales of Mother Goose* (*Les Contes de ma Mère l'Oye*) in 1697. Perrault drew his inspiration from traditional folktales and contemporary references as a fashionable courtier. The castle in "Sleeping Beauty" is based, for example, on the fantastically turreted Château d'Ussé in the Loire region, and the model for the Marquis of Carabas in "Puss in Boots" was the sixteenth-century courtier Claude Gouffier, who had the title of the Marquis de Caravaz.[231]

🐚 The novel *La Disparition* (1969) by Georges Perec has no occurrence of the letter *E* except in the author's name.

🐚 A palindrome is a text that reads the same backward as forward. The longest palindrome of all time is in French and was written by Georges Perec. It runs to 1,247 words.[232]

🐚 The longest sentence in French literature runs to 847 words and is found in the notoriously prolix novel by Marcel Proust, *À la recherche du temps perdu* (*Remembrance of Things Past*, 1913). It narrowly beats a sentence of 823 words in Victor Hugo's 1862 novel *Les Misérables*. The record for the longest sentence in English literature was until recently held by James Joyce and appeared in his novel *Ulysses* (4,391 words), but has been surpassed by a sentence of 13,955 words in *The Rotters' Club* by Jonathan Coe.[233]

## The Longest Sentence in French Literature

### (*from Volume 4 of* À la recherche du temps perdu— Sodom et Gomorrhe)[234]

*Their honor precarious, their liberty provisional, lasting only until the discovery of their crime; their position unstable, like that of the poet who one day was feasted at every table, applauded in every theater in London, and on the*

*next was driven from every lodging, unable to find a pillow
upon which to lay his head, turning the mill like Samson
and saying like him: "The two sexes shall die, each in a
place apart!"; excluded even, save on the days of general
disaster when the majority rally round the victim as the Jews
rallied round Dreyfus, from the sympathy—at times from
the society—of their fellows, in whom they inspire only
disgust at seeing themselves as they are, portrayed in a
mirror which, ceasing to flatter them, accentuates every
blemish that they have refused to observe in themselves, and
makes them understand that what they have been calling
their love (a thing to which, playing upon the word, they
have by association annexed all that poetry, painting,
music, chivalry, asceticism have contrived to add to love)
springs not from an ideal of beauty which they have chosen
but from an incurable malady; like the Jews again (save
some who will associate only with others of their race and
have always on their lips ritual words and consecrated
pleasantries), shunning one another, seeking out those who
are most directly their opposite, who do not desire their
company, pardoning their rebuffs, moved to ecstasy by their
condescension; but also brought into the company of their
own kind by the ostracism that strikes them, the opprobrium
under which they have fallen, having finally been invested,
by a persecution similar to that of Israel, with the physical
and moral characteristics of a race, sometimes beautiful,
often hideous, finding (in spite of all the mockery with which
he who, more closely blended with, better assimilated to
the opposing race, is relatively, in appearance, the least*

*inverted, heaps upon him who has remained more so) a
relief in frequenting the society of their kind, and even some
corroboration of their own life, so much so that, while
steadfastly denying that they are a race (the name of which
is the vilest of insults), those who succeed in concealing the
fact that they belong to it they readily unmask, with a view
less to injuring them, though they have no scruple about
that, than to excusing themselves; and, going in search (as
a doctor seeks cases of appendicitis) of cases of inversion in
history, taking pleasure in recalling that Socrates was one of
themselves, as the Israelites claim that Jesus was one of
them, without reflecting that there were no abnormals when
homosexuality was the norm, no anti-Christians before
Christ, that the disgrace alone makes the crime because it
has allowed to survive only those who remained obdurate to
every warning, to every example, to every punishment, by
virtue of an innate disposition so peculiar that it is more
repugnant to other men (even though it may be accompanied
by exalted moral qualities) than certain other vices which
exclude those qualities, such as theft, cruelty, breach of
faith, vices better understood and so more readily excused by
the generality of men; forming a freemasonry far more
extensive, more powerful and less suspected than that of the
Lodges, for it rests upon an identity of tastes, needs, habits,
dangers, apprenticeship, knowledge, traffic, glossary, and
one in which the members themselves, who intend not to
know one another, recognize one another immediately by
natural or conventional, involuntary or deliberate signs
which indicate one of his congeners to the beggar in the*

street, in the great nobleman whose carriage door he is
shutting, to the father in the suitor for his daughter's hand,
to him who has sought healing, absolution, defense, in the
doctor, the priest, the barrister to whom he has had recourse;
all of them obliged to protect their own secret but having
their part in a secret shared with the others, which the rest of
humanity does not suspect and which means that to them
the most wildly improbable tales of adventure seem true, for
in this romantic, anachronistic life the ambassador is a
bosom friend of the felon, the prince, with a certain independence of action with which his aristocratic breeding has
furnished him, and which the trembling little cit would lack,
on leaving the duchess's party goes off to confer in private
with the hooligan; a reprobate part of the human whole, but
an important part, suspected where it does not exist, flaunt-
ing itself, insolent and unpunished, where its existence is
never guessed; numbering its adherents everywhere, among
the people, in the army, in the church, in the prison, on the
throne; living, in short, at least to a great extent, in a
playful and perilous intimacy with the men of the other
race, provoking them, playing with them by speaking of its
vice as of something alien to it; a game that is rendered easy
by the blindness or duplicity of the others, a game that may
be kept up for years until the day of the scandal, on which
these lion-tamers are devoured; until then, obliged to make
a secret of their lives, to turn away their eyes from the things
on which they would naturally fasten them, to fasten them
upon those from which they would naturally turn away, to
change the gender of many of the words in their vocabulary,

> *a social constraint, slight in comparison with the inward*
> *constraint which their vice, or what is improperly so called,*
> *imposes upon them with regard not so much now to others as*
> *to themselves, and in such a way that to themselves it does*
> *not appear a vice.*

♔ The longest novel ever written is the French book *Artamène ou le Grand Cyrus* by Madeleine de Scudéry, a seventeenth-century romance that runs to 2.1 million words in ten volumes. The book is credited to Georges Scudéry, but is generally believed to have been written by his sister, Madeleine.

## The top ten longest novels of all time are:

1. *Artamène ou le Grand Cyrus* by Georges/Madeleine de Scudéry (1649–1653), 2,100,000 words: Romance in the *roman héroïque* form.

2. *À la recherche du temps perdu (Remembrance of Things Past)* by Marcel Proust (1913), 1,267,069 words: Proust's epic doorstop about time and memory.

3. *Mission Earth* by L. Ron Hubbard (1985–1987), 1,200,000 words: Ten-book series by the founder of Scientology, billed as a "satirical science fiction adventure set in the far future." It has been panned by critics and attempts have even been made to ban it. The town of Dalton, Georgia, for example, tried to have it removed from its public library on the basis of what it

claimed were "repeated passages involving chronic masochism, child abuse, homosexuality, necromancy, bloody murder, and other things that are anti-social, perverted, and anti-everything."

4. *Der Mann Ohne Eigenschaften* (*The Man Without Qualities*) by Robert Musil (1940), 1,774 pages: A "story of ideas" that takes place in the last days of the Austro-Hungarian Empire in 1913. Musil never completed it.

5. *Zettels Traum* by Arno Schmidt (1970), 1,100,000 words: A book about the problems of translating the works of Edgar Allan Poe into German.

6. *Min Kamp* (*My Struggle*) by Karl Ove Knausgård (2009–2011), 1,000,000 words: Not *that* book, but an autobiographical work by a Norwegian author that became notorious for its stark portrayal of the gritty details of the author's life.

7. *Clarissa, or the History of a Young Lady* by Samuel Richardson (1748), 984,870 words: an epistolary novel (i.e., a novel written as a series of letters) that tells the tragic story of a heroine on an endless and hopeless task for virtue.

8. *Joseph und seine brüder* (*Joseph and His Brothers*) by Thomas Mann (1943), 1,492 pages: A massive tome retelling the

classic tales of Genesis within the context of ancient
Egypt.

9. *Kelidar* by Mahmud Doulatabadi (1984), 950,000 words:
The story of a Kurdish family set against the backdrop of
the Second World War.

10. *Ponniyin Selvan* (*The Son of Ponni*) by Kalki Krishna-
murthy (150s), 900,000 words: A Tamil novel about one
of the kings of the Chola dynasty.[235]

# M Is for...

## ...Mata Hari

The legendary Dutch dancer and spy Mata Hari (real name: Margaretha Geertruida Zelle, 1876–1917), was executed in France for alleged espionage during the First World War. Hari was married to a Scotsman in the Dutch colonial army, Captain Campbell McLeod. She lived with him in Java and Sumatra, where she developed an interest in East Indian dance. After their divorce she moved to Paris, where she used her full figure to its fullest advantage, dancing in the nude at various venues. She also changed her name from the rather prosaic Lady McLeod to the much more exotic Mata Hari, the Malay expression for "eye of the sun." After allegedly spying first on the Germans for the French and then on the French for the Germans, Mata Hari was arrested, tried, and sentenced to death by the French (although there were claims the trial was rigged). She proclaimed her innocence in court by screaming: "Harlot, yes! But traitoress, *never!*"

Hari was executed by firing squad on October 15, 1917. Her last words, uttered to a nun, reflected the mysticism of her adopted name: "Death is nothing, nor life either, for that matter. To die, to sleep, to pass into nothingness, what does it matter? Everything is an illusion." After her death, Mata Hari's head was embalmed and kept at the Museum of Anatomy in Paris. However, in 2000 the museum archivists discovered that the head had disappeared, possibly when the museum was relocated in 1954. Mata Hari's other remains had also disappeared, and were never accounted for.[236]

## ...Merde

♕ France's capital city, Paris, is renowned for canine deposits on its sidewalks. The infamy has some justification. The city's 300,000-strong dog population drops about 20 tons of dog poop on its sidewalks every year, which amounts to two pounds of *merde* hitting the walkways every five seconds (enough to fill three Olympic swimming pools).[237]

♕ The French word *merde* does, literally, mean "s***." However, it is used by the French as a mild swear word and NOT to describe dog poop on a Paris sidewalk. The French would refer to the latter as *crottes de chien*. The French often also refer to *merde* as *le mot de Cambronne*. This is a reference to General Pierre Cambronne (1770–1842), who, when called upon by the British to surrender at the Battle of Waterloo in 1815, is said to have replied with the single, forceful retort: "*Merde!*"[238]

♕ While English actors wish each other luck by saying "break a leg," French actors are more likely to wish each other "*Merde!*" Why? It is believed that the origins of this usage date to the days of horse-drawn carriages. A successful play would result in long lines of horses and carriages at the entrance to the theater . . . with the inevitable deposits on the sidewalk.[239]

## ...Misnomers & Misunderstandings

✼ French toast was not invented in France, but is believed to have originated in Roman times. The first reference to French toast in the English language is in a cookbook of 1660 by a certain R. May called *Accomplisht Cook*, with the following directions: "French Toasts. Cut French Bread, and toast it in pretty thick toasts on a gridiron, and serve them steeped in claret, sack, or any wine, with sugar and juyce of orange." It appears, therefore, that the appellation "French" came from the practice of using French bread to make the toast, rather than the actual *technique* of frying in egg and milk. In any event, on no account attempt to ask for *toast à la française* in a French restaurant, unless you wish to receive a blank stare. The proper French term is *pain perdu* ("lost bread").[240]

✼ The world-famous French breakfast pastry, the croissant, was actually invented in Austria. Its early ancestor was a form of Austrian pastry called the *kipferl*. It was brought to Paris by the Austrian August Zang, who set up a Viennese bakery on the rue de Richelieu in Paris in 1839. Zang didn't hang about after reinventing the French *petit déjeuner*: having introduced *viennoiserie* to France, he went back to Vienna to found the newspaper *Die Presse*. The word "croissant" actually derives from the "crescent" shape of the pastry, reminiscent of a waxing moon.[241]

✼ The soft cheese Petit Suisse comes from Normandy in northern France, and not Switzerland. The name "Suisse" comes from the fact that the cheese was created in the 1850s at the suggestion of a young Swiss lad, an employee of a farm in Normandy, to add cream to the cheese produced at the farm.[242]

♕ Foie gras, the quintessentially French pâté made from duck or goose livers, originated in ancient Egypt. The practice of *gavage*—or force-feeding of birds—dates as far back as 2500 BC, when the Egyptians began keeping birds for food and sacrifice and deliberately fattened them by force-feeding.[243]

♕ The French manicure—or technique of painting nails with a nude or natural finish and white tips—was probably invented by a Hollywood beautician, Jeff Pink, in the 1970s. Pink claims that he invented the technique to enable Hollywood stars to change their wardrobes between scenes easily, without having to change their nail polish; and that he later took his invention to Paris, christening it the "French" manicure. Others claim that the early French manicure was invented by Polish-Jewish beautician Max Factor in the 1930s, for the fashionistas of the Paris catwalks.[244]

♕ The celebrated leek-and-potato soup vichyssoise (traditionally served cold) is not a traditional French recipe, but dates from the twentieth century and is probably of American origin. The chef most frequently credited with its invention is Louis Diat, a French chef at the Ritz-Carlton in New York City. Diat told *The New Yorker* in 1950:

"In the summer of 1917, when I had been at the Ritz seven years, I reflected upon the potato and leek soup of my childhood which my mother and grandmother used to make. I recalled how during the summer my older brother and I used to cool it off by pouring in cold milk and how delicious it was. I resolved to make something of the sort for the patrons of the Ritz."

Diat called his soup vichyssoise, after the French town of Vichy, near his hometown. The American chef, author, and TV personality Julia Child called vichyssoise "an American invention."[245]

☙ The brass instrument known as the French horn probably originated in Germany. It derived from early forms of hunting horns. The International Horn Society refuses to use the "misleading" term *French horn*, and refers to the instrument instead as simply "the horn." This is largely due to the efforts of the first editor of the British magazine *Horn Call*, Harold Meek, which stated in every issue: "The International Horn Society recommends that HORN be recognized as the correct name for our instrument in the English language."[246]

☙ The breed of dog known as the French bulldog (or "Frenchie") originated from small bulldogs imported into France from England in the late eighteenth and early nineteenth centuries. The dogs became a fashionable craze in Paris, leading to the addition of "French" to the breed's nomenclature.[247]

☙ The precise origins of so-called French fries is a subject of much debate, but the general view is that fries as we know them were most probably invented in Belgium. The earliest known reference to French fries in English literature is in Charles Dickens's *A Tale of Two Cities* (1859), which refers to "husky chips of potato, fried with some reluctant drops of oil." The American president Thomas Jefferson was the first to introduce French fries to the United States, having requested "potatoes served in the French manner" for a dinner at the White House in 1802. The world's only museum dedicated to French fries is the Frietmuseum in Bruges, Belgium.[248]

The renaming of French fries as "Freedom fries" during the

Iraq War is just one, but perhaps the most notorious, case of food being renamed for political reasons. Other, lesser known, examples include:

- *Kiwi Loaves*: In 1998, in protest of French nuclear tests in the Pacific Ocean, New Zealand bakers rechristened French bread "Kiwi loaves."
- *Liberty Hounds*: During the Second World War, rather than risk any association with the enemy, pet owners replaced the Teutonic breed names of their German shepherds and dachshunds with the appellations "Alsatians" and "Liberty Hounds."
- *Liberty Measles*: In a bid to take the battle against the Huns to its limits in World War I, a Massachusetts doctor rechristened German measles "Liberty measles"—a term that caught on in the media.
- *Liberty Cabbage*: Again during World War I, German sauerkraut was renamed "Liberty Cabbage."
- *Roses of Muhammad*: After the 2006 debacle over Danish cartoons depicting the Prophet Muhammad, the Iranian Confectioners' Union changed the name of Danish pastries to "Roses of the Prophet Muhammad."
- *Mecca Cola*: In 2002, a Muslim beverage company introduced "Mecca Cola" as an alternative to Coca-Cola. Sales were boosted by the then-ongoing Arab boycott of American brands.[249]

🐚 The notorious derogatory phrase for the French—"cheese-eating surrender monkeys"—first appeared in 1995 in the television series *The Simpsons*. School janitor Groundskeeper

Willie, unexpectedly tasked with teaching a French class at Springfield Elementary School as a result of budget cuts, addressed the class with the greeting, "Bonjour, you cheese-eating surrender monkeys." Since the day it was first uttered, the phrase has been endlessly repeated as a staple in the stock arsenal of insults against the French, notably in the run-up to the Iraq War. It was in particular popularized in 2003, when it was used by the conservative American columnist Jonathan Goldberg to attack French opposition to the invasion of Iraq. Interestingly, if you mention the phrase to a French person, he or she will look at you blankly. This is because the voiceover was modified to "cheese-eating monkeys" (*singes mangeurs de fromage*) when the episode was broadcast in France.[250]

👑 The origins of the traditional derogatory term of the French for the English—*les Rosbifs* ("roast beefs")—are shrouded in mystery. It is presumed to have originated from the English preference for roast beef as a dish. Englishmen were traditionally associated with the color red, from the color of Wellington's "redcoats" at the Battle of Waterloo. A more unkind association is probably an allusion to the color of the average Englishman after exposure to the sun. The French have many mean names for the English complexion, including *tête d'endives* ("chicory heads"), a comparison based on the fact that chicory is cultivated in the dark to preserve the whiteness of the leaves.[251]

👑 The French company Bich (French pronunciation *Bik*) changed its name to *Bic* in the 1940s, to stop people in English-speaking countries pronouncing it "bitch." As an inverse exercise in rebranding, the Toyota MR2 car (pronounced *em-er-deux* in French) is referred to as just the *MR* in

France, because of the connotations with the word *merdeux* ("shitty").[252]

♕ The song "My Way," made famous by the crooner Frank Sinatra, was in fact originally a French song, "*Comme d'habitude*," sung by the French pop star Claude François (1939–1978). Dubbed "Cloclo" by his adoring public and famous for his signature blond flick-and-glitter suits, François died an untimely death when he was electrocuted in the shower at the age of thirty-nine.[253]

[See also *La Marseillaise*, under the heading *France*].


## …Mona Lisa

♕ Many people wonder how the *Mona Lisa*—a painting identified very much with the Italian Renaissance—made its way to France. The answer is that its creator, Leonardo da Vinci (1452–1519), made Château du Clos Lucé in Amboise, France, his home from 1516 until his death. The painting was purchased, after da Vinci's death, from his assistant, Salai, by King François I. The French refer to the *Mona Lisa* as *La Joconde* (after the fact that the likely subject of the portrait, Lisa Gherardini, was the wife of one Francesco del Giocondo).

The question most frequently asked at the inquiry desk of the Louvre Museum in Paris is: *Where is the* Mona Lisa? Next comes: *Where am I?* Of the other great treasures of the Louvre, the whereabouts of only the Venus de Milo is commonly requested.[254]

꘎ The *Mona Lisa* is referred to by staff and employees at the Louvre as *Painting No. 779.*[255]

꘎ The *Mona Lisa* is the painting most widely used in advertising in the world. The smile of *La Joconde* has been used to sell laxatives, Spanish oranges, condoms, Air India flights to Paris, Doncella cigars, Rembrandt toothpaste (somewhat confusing Old Masters), Italian air-conditioning equipment (featured clad in a woolen scarf and earmuffs), wigs, a dental prosthesis, and a blood-testing kit for Hepatitis B. According to art historian and critic Donald Sassoon, since 1980 there has been a new utilization of the *Mona Lisa* in advertising every week.[256]

꘎ In the 1980s, a stockbroker named Léon Mekusa made the headlines as a result of selling his firm to take a job as a Louvre guard. He explained his actions by stating that it was such a joy to greet Lisa every morning that he had asked not to be paid.[257]

꘎ A much lesser-known Mona Lisa, but equally bound up with the history of Paris, is the so-called *Mona Lisa of the Seine* (or *L'Inconnue de la Seine*). In the late 1880s, the body of a teenage girl, her eyes closed, was pulled out of the River Seine. The story goes that the pathologist at the Paris morgue was so taken by her beauty that he cast her face in wax. The cast was swiftly copied and became a morbid decorative fixture in the studios of Parisian artists at the turn of the century. Albert Camus possessed one, and compared her beatific smile with that of the *Mona Lisa*. Over the years Rilke, Louis Aragon, Man Ray, and Vladimir Nabokov successively fell under the *Inconnue*'s spell, and at one time no fashionable European drawing room was complete without her mask on the wall. The critic Al Alvarez wrote in his book on suicide, *The Savage God*: "I am told that a whole generation of German girls modelled their looks on her."

*L'Inconnue*'s story was given a bizarre twist in 1955 when the Norwegian toy manufacturer Asmund Laerdal was looking to develop a training doll for the newly developed technique of CPR. Recalling the *Inconnue* mask that had hung on the wall of his parents' home when he was a child, Laerdal modeled the face of his new training doll, Resusci Anne, on *L'Inconnue*. The fact that the mannequin has since been used to train over 300 million emergency first-aid students has resulted in hers having been called "the most kissed face" of all time.[258]

☙ While the *Mona Lisa* by the Italian da Vinci may be the most famous painting in the world, the most expensive is by a French artist. *When Will You Marry?*—a portrait of two Tahitian women by the post-Impressionist painter Paul Gauguin—broke all previous records when it was reportedly sold for $300 million to the Qatar Museums in 2015.[259]

# N Is for...

## ...Napoleon

In the first French edition of George Orwell's *Animal Farm*, the pig-dictator who is the lead villain—named Napoleon in the original, after the French leader Napoleon Bonaparte (1769–1821)*— was rechristened César, leading to the widely believed urban myth that it is illegal in France to call a pig Napoleon. Later translations have restored the character's name to Napoleon.[260]

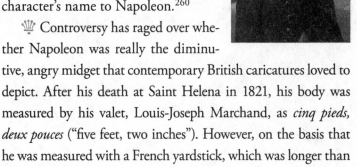

Controversy has raged over whether Napoleon was really the diminutive, angry midget that contemporary British caricatures loved to depict. After his death at Saint Helena in 1821, his body was measured by his valet, Louis-Joseph Marchand, as *cinq pieds, deux pouces* ("five feet, two inches"). However, on the basis that he was measured with a French yardstick, which was longer than the British yardstick, some historians have argued that he was in fact five feet, six inches tall (the French foot equals 33 cm, the

---

*The French refer to Napoleon Bonaparte (1769–1821) as Napoleon I, to distinguish him from his successors.

British 30.47 cm). Whatever the truth of the matter, the myth of Napoleon's diminutive height has stuck. So much so that there is even a controversial psychological condition known as the Napoleon complex. This is defined as overly aggressive or domineering behavior, intended to compensate for shortness of stature.[261]

The most expensive weapon ever sold is a gold encrusted sword used by Napoleon in battle two hundred years ago. The sword brought in €4.8 million ($6.5 million) at an auction in Fontainebleau, France, in 2007. It is thought the sword was used by Napoleon in battle at Marengo in June 1800, before he became emperor.

## The Top Five Most Expensive Weapons in the World are:

1. Napoleon's sword, as above—$6.5 million.

2. Eighteenth-century Chinese jade-hilted sword—$5.9 million. A ceremonial steel-bladed sword, produced during the reign of the Qianlong emperor from 1736 to 1795, sold at Sotheby's Hong Kong in 2006.

3. Shah Jahan's gold dagger—$3.3 million. Bonhams in London sold a gold dagger that was owned by Shah Jahan (1592–1666), the Mughal emperor who built the Taj Mahal, in April 2008.

4. Pair of steel-mounted "saddle" pistols owned by George Washington—$2 million. These pistols, marked by Jacob Walster, were owned by President George Washington during America's Revolutionary War. They were also linked

to the Marquis de Lafayette and, later, to seventh U.S. president Andrew Jackson. Sold at Christie's in New York in 2002.

5. Pair of Nicolas-Noël Boutet flintlock pistols owned by Simón Bolívar—$1.8 million. Sold in November 2004 at Christie's, New York.[262]

꧁ After his final defeat at the Battle of Waterloo, Napoleon was exiled far away, to the tropical island of Saint Helena in the South Atlantic, where he lived until his death in 1821 at the age of fifty-one. There have been myriad stated causes of his death, from cancer to scurvy to syphilis, but perhaps the most curious is the theory that he was killed by his wallpaper. Tests on pieces of wallpaper in Longwood House, in which Napoleon died, revealed large amounts of arsenic (as was common in wallpaper in those days), and arsenic was also found in locks of his hair. On the other hand, he could simply have been murdered by arsenic—a favorite weapon of the poisoner at the time.[263]

꧁ Napoleon's last words, uttered on his deathbed, are said to have been: "France . . . army . . . head of the army . . . Joséphine* . . ." (in that order).[264]

꧁ While there are over two hundred streets, squares, and monuments in Paris that record the accomplishments and victories of Napoleon and his generals, there is no monument actually named after Napoleon himself. There is, however, a statue of Napoleon on top of a column at Paris's Place Vendôme, in the 1st arrondissement.

---

*Referring to Joséphine de Beauharnais (1763–1814), Napoleon's mistress for many years and, later, his wife.

# O Is for...

## ...Oysters

**Types and sizes of French oysters**

Oysters in France can by flat or cupped, but the choice is often limited as 98 percent of French oysters are cupped. French oysters are numbered by shell size, from 0 (smallest) to 5 (largest) for cupped oysters, and 000 (smallest) to 6 (largest) for flat oysters. For cupped oysters, the indication *spéciale* denotes the meatiest varieties.

The flavor of French oysters varies greatly according to the region in which they are farmed. *Normandy* oysters (including the celebrated Utah Beach oysters) are highly iodized in flavor, while those of *Brittany* are highly oxygenated, salty, and firm yet soft. The center of oyster production in France is *Marennes-Oléron*, and oysters are also farmed in *Aquitaine*.

Unique to French oyster production is the final maturing of oysters in shallow, mixed seawater and freshwater beds, earning them the special *appellations* of *fines de claire* and *spéciales de claire*.[265]

## Legendary Oyster Lovers

- Casanova—50 oysters before one of his notorious amatory exploits
- Balzac—100 oysters for lunch
- Bismarck—150 oysters for dinner
- Louis XIV—400 oysters before his wedding night
- Emperor Aulus Vitellius—1,000 oysters at a banquet[266]

The high season for oysters is the winter season, leading to the long-held saying that oysters (in common with mussels) should only be eaten in months with an *R* (i.e., January, February, March, April, September, October, November, and December).

# P Is for...

## ...Paris

♛ Paris is the fifth-most visited city in the world. The top ranking cities for visitors are: 1. Hong Kong (25.6 million visits), 2. Singapore (22.5 million visits), 3. Bangkok (17.5 million visits), 4. London (16.8 million visits), and 5. Paris (15.2 million visits).[267]

✍ The famous moniker for Paris—"City of Light"—originally referred to its being the center of the Enlightenment in the seventeenth and eighteenth centuries. Later, the term was applied more literally, as Paris was one of the first European cities to introduce gas streetlights in the nineteenth century.[268]

✍ Paris is the fifth-ranked bike-sharing city in the world, with the *Velib* (system of street bikes for hire) continuing its immense popularity. The full ranking is: 1. Hangzhou, China (78,000 bikes), 2. Wuhan, China (70,000 bikes), 3. Tiayuan, China (35,000 bikes), 4. Taizhou, China (24,225 bikes), and 5. Paris, France (23,900 bikes).[269]

✍ The twenty arrondissements, or municipal districts, of Paris are arranged in a circular snail shape, starting with the 1st on the inside right bank of the city, and spiraling outward. The number of the arrondissement is indicated by the last two digits of Parisian postal codes, with the starting code "75" standing for Paris, from 75001 to 75020.

✍ "Paris syndrome" is defined as a psychosis triggered by a visit to the City of Light. It is characterized by an acute delusional state, persecution complex, hallucinations, and panic attacks. Apparently, this is an affliction to which Japanese tourists in Paris are particularly susceptible, resulting in the hospitalization of several dozen a year. The condition is thought to be brought on by the highly idealized vision of Paris entertained by the average Japanese visitor, which is shattered by the reality of the experience. The Japanese embassy in Paris has a 24-hour hotline for Japanese visitors in the throes of this reality crisis, and a department of the Parisian Hospital of St. Anne is devoted to caring for its victims as well as to the study of this curious condition.[270]

Cities other than Paris that have given their name to a syndrome include:

- *Stockholm syndrome*: the condition whereby a kidnapped person develops empathy for the kidnapper (named after a bank robbery in Sweden during which a female bank employee developed a strong attachment to her captor).[271]
- *Jerusalem syndrome*: religious delusions as a result of a visit to the city of Jerusalem.[272]
- *London syndrome*: the inverse of Stockholm Syndrome—when the kidnapper and hostage have an antagonistic relationship.[273]
- *Florence syndrome/Stendhal syndrome*: extreme hallucinations as a result of overexposure to works of art.[274]

♕ There is only one stop sign in the city of Paris, in the 16th arrondissement, on the quay St-Exupéry.[275]

♕ The Louvre museum in Paris is the most visited museum in the world, with 9.7 million visitors in 2012 (the equivalent of the entire population of Sweden).[276]

♕ According to a 2010 survey, Paris was voted by travelers as Europe's worst smelling city. (The worst smelling city in the world was voted as Bangkok, Thailand.)[277]

♕ While Paris has pacts of cooperation with a number of cities around the world, only Rome has the distinction of being its sister city. Paris and Rome entered into an exclusive sister city relationship in 1956. There is a French saying that goes: "*Seule Paris est digne de Rome; seule Rome est digne de Paris*"

("Only Paris is worthy of Rome; only Rome is worthy of Paris").[278]

⚜ The oldest bridge in Paris is the Pont Neuf ("New Bridge"). The bridge was completed during the reign of Henri IV and inaugurated in 1607. It spans both Right and Left Banks, connecting them to the central island in the Seine, the Isle de la Cité. The bridge came to be known as a center of teeming city life, with jugglers, beggars, street vendors, and even its own gallows. In 1701, the French writer Charles Cotolendi quoted a letter said to have been written by a Sicilian tourist:

> One finds on the Pont-Neuf an infinity of people who give tickets, some put fallen teeth back in, and others make crystal eyes; there are those who cure incurable illnesses; those who claim to have discovered the virtues of some powdered stones to white and to beautify the face. This one claims he makes old men young; there are those who remove wrinkles from the forehead and the eyes, who make wooden legs to repair the violence of bombs; finally everybody is so applied to work, so strongly and continually, that the devil can tempt no one but on Holidays and Sundays.[279]

⚜ The world's first department store was founded by Aristide Boucicaut in Paris, in 1838. The store, Le Bon Marché, became a center for innovation and the development of modern shopping concepts including advertisements, browsing, and fixed prices. Boucicaut has been hailed as a genius, introducing the nineteenth-century middle-class woman to the fantasyland of shopping and the dream world of luxury goods. Today, Le Bon Marché still stands on the Left Bank of Paris, and is known as one of Paris's most exclusive department stores.[280]

☙ There is a one-fourth scale replica of the Statue of Liberty in Paris, on an island in the Seine called Île aux Cygnes ("Island of the Swans"). The statue was given as a gift by the American community of Paris to the Parisians in 1889, in commemoration of the centenary of the French Revolution. The statue of the Île aux Cygnes carries a joint inscription commemorating both American Independence Day and Bastille Day, the defining moment of the French Revolution:

*IV Juillet 1776 = XIV Juillet 1789*

In fact, France boasts more replicas of the Statue of Liberty than any other country. Paris is home to four. In addition to the statue on Île aux Cygnes, the bronze model used by the sculptor, Frédéric Auguste Bartholdi, as a study for the New York statue stands in the Luxembourg Gardens; a plaster version is displayed in the Paris Arts and Crafts Museum; and a life-size copy of Liberty's torch can be seen at the entrance to the Pont d'Alma tunnel. Copies of Liberty gaze down on French citizens in regional cities as far-flung as Bordeaux, Barentin, Colmar, Saint-Cyr-sur-Mer, Poitiers, Châteauneuf-la-Forêt, and Lunel.[281]

☙ Very few people know that there is a vineyard in Paris, right behind the Sacré-Coeur. In fact, there was a time when the Île-de-France region was the most important wine-producing area in the entire country. Nowadays, Clos Montmartre still produces about 1,700 bottles of wine a year, but the wine can't be found in the shops. The best time to track it down is during the annual wine festival, or Fête des Vendanges, at Montmartre.

🐚 All the trees in Paris have been counted and measured: there are 470,000 in total.[282]

🐚 The bell of Notre-Dame cathedral weighs over 13 tons and is called Emmanuel.[283]

🐚 There are over two dozen towns, census-designated places, or other unincorporated communities in the United States named Paris:

- Paris, Arkansas
- Paris, Idaho
- Paris, Illinois
- Paris, Indiana
- Paris, Iowa
- Paris, Kentucky
- Paris, Maine
- Paris, Michigan
- Paris, Mississippi
- Paris, Missouri
- Paris, New York
- Paris, Ohio
- Paris, Oregon*
- Paris, Pennsylvania
- Paris, Tennessee
- Paris, Texas§

---

*Not named after Paris, France, but GE Parris, the town's first postmaster.
§ Most famous for a film—*Paris, Texas* by German director Wim Wenders—which is not actually set there.

- Paris, Virginia
- Paris, Grant County, Wisconsin
- Paris, Kenosha County, Wisconsin
- Paris Township, Michigan
- New Paris, Indiana
- New Paris, Ohio
- New Paris, Pennsylvania
- New Paris, Wisconsin
- South Paris, Maine
- West Paris, Maine

American cities named Paris follow a tradition of erecting a replica of the Eiffel Tower. The one in Paris, Texas, is famously topped by a red cowboy hat.

## ...Perfume

The most iconic French perfume of all time, according to a survey by *Vogue* magazine in 2014, is the classic Chanel N°5. Launched in the 1920s by Coco Chanel, the fragrance was created by Chanel's pharmacist, Ernest Beaux, perfumer to the Russian tsars. Beaux presented his sample perfumes to Chanel in numbered bottles, and she chose the fifth bottle. The number 5 had always held a mystical significance for Coco Chanel, partly because the paths around the cathedral of the convent in which she had grown up were arranged in concentric circles, repeating the number 5. When it appeared, the rose and jasmine scents of Chanel N°5—combined with a "clean winter note" produced by Beaux' groundbreaking use of synthetic ingredients—was a radical departure from the heavier, floral scents of previous women's perfumes. The classically simple glass bottle—inspired, allegedly, by the whiskey bottle preferred by Chanel's then lover, Arthur "Boy" Capel—also broke with the traditions of the past, the more ornate and fussy perfume bottles produced by the likes of Lalique and Baccarat. Coco Chanel was later to say of the perfume: "That is what I was waiting for. A perfume like nothing else. A woman's perfume, with the scent of a woman."[284]

⚜ The second-most famous French perfume, after Chanel N°5, is probably Guerlain's Shalimar. The original Shalimar bottle (Bottle #597) was designed by Baccarat for Jacques Guerlain in 1925. Shalimar was the first commercially sold "oriental" fragrance, with notes of bergamot, jasmine, and iris ("oriental," or spicy, fragrances, were previously considered the preserve of prostitutes and not worn by "nice" women). In creating the perfume, Guerlain was inspired by Mumtaz Mahal, the beloved wife of Shah Jahan, for whom the Moghul emperor designed the Shalimar gardens in Lahore, Pakistan (along with the more famous Taj Mahal). When Shalimar first appeared in 1925, the whole of Paris was entranced by the exotic: it was the year when the African American dancer Josephine Baker first entered La Revue Nègre on the Champs-Élysées, with her feverish "Danse Sauvage." The musky notes of Shalimar shocked and delighted the public, and for many years the scent was considered decidedly risqué. As the 1920s saying went: "There are three things no respectable woman should do: smoke, dance the tango, and wear Shalimar . . ."[285]

⚜ The current favorite perfume of French women is Christian Dior's scent J'Adore. Since 2011, this has headed the perfume charts in France, with 826,000 bottles sold in 2013.

J'Adore is followed in the rankings by Lancôme's La vie est belle ("Life Is Beautiful"), and in third place, Guerlain's La petite robe noire ("Little Black Dress").[286]

[See also entry for the perfumer Fragonard under subject heading *Fragonard*].

## ...President

♛ The French president Félix Faure (1841–1899) has the distinction of being the only (known) head of state to have died in the throes of an orgasm. The story has it that Faure was having oral sex performed on him by his mistress, Marguerite Steinheil, when he suffered a fatal heart attack. The alarm was sounded, only for the president to be discovered on a couch, his naked mistress attempting to disentangle her hair from his clothes. The cause of death was said to be a "cerebral hemorrhage" caused by "strong emotion." The French slang word for oral sex being *pomper* ("to pump"), various unkind jokes were made on his death, including by his archrival, French prime minister Georges Clemenceau, who remarked *Il voulait être César, mais il ne fut que Pompey* ("He wanted to be Caesar, but he ended up as Pompey/being 'pumped' "). Steinheil herself seemed to be pursued by drama. In May 1908, she was found bound and gagged in her bed, her then husband strangled and her mother dead of a heart attack. Arrested for the crime, she was subsequently acquitted. She eventually married an English baron and died, at the age of eighty-five years, in the sedate English county of Sussex.[287]

♛ The president of France in 1920, Paul Deschanel, served

only seven months and—despite being a great intellect and member of the Académie Française—became completely mad once he assumed the presidential office. His eccentric behavior was the cause of considerable consternation. Once, for example, when a delegation of schoolgirls presented him with a bouquet, he threw the flowers back at them, one by one. On another occasion, he received the British ambassador stark naked, save for the sash and collar of the Légion d'honneur. The last straw was during one night in May 1920, when he fell out of the window of the presidential train in his pajamas. He was discovered wandering by the tracks, and taken for shelter to the home of a nearby crossing guard. He later walked out of a state meeting straight into a lake, with all his clothes still on him. He resigned in September 1920, due to mental health issues.[288]

♛ The French president Charles de Gaulle survived the most assassination attempts—thirty-one—of any president in the world. Most of the attempts were by the OAS (Secret Army Organization). The most famous attempt was by a lone sniper, immortalized in the Frederick Forsyth book and subsequent film *Day of the Jackal*.[289]

# Q Is for...

## ...Queen

♛ Perhaps the most famous and certainly the most unfortunate of French queens is the doomed wife of Louis XVI, Marie-Antoinette (1755–1793). Born in Vienna as an Austrian princess, she was only fourteen years old when she was married to the future Louis XVI. The marriage was unconsummated for seven years, because Louis had an erectile dysfunction that required surgery. He was finally persuaded by the Emperor Joseph II—who referred to the couple as "complete blunderers"—to have the necessary procedures, and the marriage was at last consummated on August 18, 1777, at ten A.M. (This was not a time when personal privacy was respected.) The queen threw a party to celebrate the event, and the following spring she was pregnant with her first child.[290]

♛ "Let them eat cake" is a comment erroneously attributed to Marie-Antoinette. The remark is the common English translation of the French "*Qu'ils mangent de la brioche.*" In fact, it appears first in Jean-Jacques Rousseau's *Confessions*, which were written when Marie-Antoinette was only nine years old. In these, the philosopher recollected the words of a "great princess" who, when told that the peasants had no bread, allegedly responded, "Let them eat brioche." As the autobiographical basis of Rousseau's work is notoriously unreliable, it is entirely possible that this immortal line is the product of the philosopher's own imagination. Moreover, it is not as thoughtless a remark as people might think. At this time, if bakers ran out of cheap bread—which was subsidized—they were obliged to sell off their more expensive products, including brioche and cake, at cheaper rates. So "Let them eat cake" may well be no more than an exhortation to bakers to feed the poor brioche at subsidized rates.[291]

꙳ Eat cake or no, the frivolities of Marie-Antoinette's court were legendary. While real peasants starved, she had a *petit hameau* ("mock-village") constructed at the Palace of Versailles, where she and her maids could dress up as shepherdesses with silver crooks and pails engraved with the royal coat of arms. One of her closest confidants was the royal hairdresser, Léonard Autié. Autié concocted the queen's gravity-defying hairdos, which could rise up to four feet high. He added poufs, feathers, and trinkets to her hair arrangements, on one occasion even perching an enormous model of the French warship *La Belle Poule* on her head, to commemorate a naval battle in which the French were victorious. The enormous constructions on the heads of the ladies of the court meant that they had to stoop in carriages, risked setting themselves on fire by coming into contact with chandeliers at the opera, and were a breeding ground for vermin. The ladies also helped spread vicious gossip about the feckless and extravagant royal couple.[292]

꙳ Nine months after the execution of Louis XVI, Marie-Antoinette was herself tried and executed on trumped-up charges of incest with her son, Louis Charles. She was brought to the scaffold as prisoner No. 280, also known as "Widow

Capet"—a name given to her by the Revolutionaries. Her last words were said to be "Monsieur, I beg your pardon," after treading on the executioner's foot (although there is some dispute as to whether this remark was genuine or sarcastic).[293]

♛ There is an American city named after Marie-Antoinette. When a group of veterans of the American Revolutionary War founded the first permanent settlement of the Northwest Territory in 1788 at the confluence of the Muskingum and Ohio Rivers, they wanted to honor France, which had been instrumental in assisting the patriots against the British. They named their new community—Marietta, Ohio—after the French queen, and even sent her a letter offering her a "public square" in the town.[294]

# R Is for...

## ...Regulations

✿ Potatoes were once illegal in France. Known as "hog feed," they were banned by the French parliament in 1748 on the basis that they caused leprosy, among other things (possibly because they are related to deadly nightshade, as are the tomato and tobacco plants). Largely due to the efforts of pioneering army pharmacist Antoine-Augustin Parmentier (1737–1813), the Paris Faculty of Medicine finally declared potatoes edible in 1772. Parmentier was a tireless promoter of the potato, hosting lavish dinner parties at which potatoes featured as the star dish. He presented the king and queen with potato flower bouquets, and placed an armed guard around his potato patch at home in Sablons, to give the impression the plants were of rare value. A number of potato-based dishes are named in honor of Parmentier, including *potage Parmentier* (potato soup) and *hachis Parmentier* (similar to shepherd's pie).[295]

✿ A French law states that no alcoholic drinks are to be permitted in the workplace other than beer, wine, cider and perry.*

✿ France was the first country to introduce the car license plate, in 1893.[297]

---

*Perry: an alcoholic beverage made of fermented pears.[296]

�™ France is the only country to require drivers to carry a portable breathalyzer in their vehicle. A person caught without this gadget may be required to pay a fine of €11 ($12) immediately (although enforcement of this fine has recently been indefinitely postponed).[298]

☙ Under French law, between eight A.M. and eight P.M., 60 percent of pop music on radio stations must be of European origin, and 40 percent in the French language.[299]

☙ A mayoral decree of the village of Lhéraule, in the Picardy area of northern France, imposes a minimum level of politeness in the town hall. The rule is that you can be thrown off the premises if you don't use basic social graces such as saying "Hello," "Thank you," and "Good-bye."[300]

## ...Religion

☙ The first French Pope was Gerbert of Aurillac, a shepherd from the Massif Central town of Aurillac. He became Sylvester II in AD 999, and introduced Arabic numerals to Western Europe.[301]

☙ The origins of the French word for Protestant dissenters—*Huguenots*—applied from the sixteenth century onward, is the subject of much debate. The prevailing theory is that it derives from the German word *eidgenossen*, meaning "confederates," or plotters united by the same ideals or objectives, under the influence of the personal name of the leader Hugues/Hugh de Besançon.[302]

☙ *Laïcité* is the French term for the separation of the Church from the State. The principle was first expressed in the 1789 Declaration of Citizens' Rights, which stated that nobody should be troubled for the expression of their opinions, unless to do so would threaten law and order. French schools have been a major vehicle for this principle, with bans on any form of religious symbolism in schools and the consecration of half a day—Wednesday afternoons—to enable school pupils to take religious instruction in their particular faith. *Laïcité* can be taken as a cardinal principle of the French state, as expressed in Article I of the French constitution: "France is a Republic that is indivisible, *laïque*, democratic, and social" (*La France est une République indivisible, laïque, démocratique et sociale*).[303]

✺ Almost two-thirds of French people declare themselves Catholic, despite the long tradition of *laïcité* in France.[304]

✺ In 2005, the municipal government of Paris passed an official law that the American actor Tom Cruise could never be made an honorary citizen. This was in connection with the actor's affiliation with Scientology, which is frowned on in France as a religious cult.[305]

✺ France has the largest Muslim population of any country of the European Union. The EU countries with the largest Muslim populations are: 1. France (4.7 million Muslims), 2. Germany (4.1 million Muslims), 3. UK (2.8 million Muslims), 4. Italy (1.5 million Muslims), and 5. Spain (1.0 million Muslims).[306]

## ...Restaurant

✺ The world's first modern restaurant was, it is claimed, founded by Monsieur Boulanger in Paris in 1765. Previously, guests at an inn would partake of a meal at a common table, but M. Boulanger's establishment introduced the innovation of

individual tables. The word *restaurant* is itself derived from the type of soup, referred to as the *bouillon restaurant* ("restorative bouillon") served at M. Boulanger's hostelry.[307]

☸ One of the oldest and most prestigious restaurants in Paris is La Tour d'Argent, an inn founded in 1582 and patronized by King Henri IV (1553–1610). Henri IV was devoted to the pleasures of the table, and promised to supply every home in France with a large black kettle. The king seldom kept his promises, but he did delight in frequenting La Tour d'Argent, so much so that he distinguished it with its very own coat of arms. The inn became a celebrated watering hole and dining spot for the Parisian elite. The first meal in France in which forks were used is supposed to have taken place there, as did a splendid feast hosted by Cardinal Richelieu's nephew, in which a whole ox was cooked in thirty different ways. In 1890 the famous ritual of the Caneton Tour d'Argent was established, every duck served in the restaurant being registered with a number in the hotel records (the total number now exceeds a million). The restaurant, with its still regal prices, exists to this day as one of the most exclusive in Paris.[308]

☸ The world's first restaurant critic was Alexandre Balthazar Laurent Grimod de la Reynière (1758–1837). Grimod introduced the first restaurant ratings service, from which contemporary guides such as Michelin and Zagat are derived. Born into an extremely wealthy family, Grimod scandalized his relatives by his dissolute living, throwing wild parties and orgies at the grand *hôtel particulier* owned by his parents in Paris. It is said that his straitlaced father was shocked one night to arrive home at one of Grimod's dinner parties, to find a pig dressed up and sitting at the head of the table. Grimod was promptly disinherited and sent to an abbey near Nancy in disgrace, where he learned from the easy-living monks to appreciate the pleasures of the table. It was shortly thereafter that he started his *Almanach des Gourmands* (1803–1812), the world's first restaurant ratings publication. Restaurants would deliver their dishes to Grimod's home, to be sampled and rated at his celebrated dinner parties. Having rescued his mother from the guillotine through his connections, Grimod was readmitted to the family fold. On her death in 1812, he moved to a grand country house, the Château de Villiers-sur-Orge, with his actress wife. There, he amused himself by inviting friends to his own funeral as a prank, and surprising houseguests with the myriad trapdoors, false walls, and other theatrical devices that he had installed at his mansion. When he died in 1837, little was left of the immense fortune he had inherited from his parents. Along with the writer and wit Jean-Anthelme Brillat-Savarin (1755–1826), famed for aphorisms such as "Tell me what you eat and I shall tell you what you are," Grimod can be considered one of the fathers of modern food journalism.[309]

꧁ The most famous French food critic of the early twentieth century was Maurice Edmond Sailland (1872–1956), aka "Curnonsky." Curnonsky had a very poetic approach to French cuisine. He described the French cheese Maroilles as "the sound of the saxophone in the symphony of French cheeses," and French fries as "the most spiritual creation of Parisian genius." He was the ultimate champion of the quintessentially French concept of *terroir*—that is, the unique link between food and the land from which it produced. Curnonsky took the idea of *terroir* to extremes—for example, he went so far as to advise never to eat the left leg of a partridge, as that is the leg it sits on, and therefore "makes the circulation sluggish." He was also partial to asking for his beef to be cooked "pink as a baby's bottom." Curnonsky was described by the American writer Gertrude Stein as a "physically amorphous creature, not dissimilar to an unfinished tub of butter." Restaurant owners would quake in their shoes to see him waiting to be served at their table, a crisp white napkin tied under his many chins. He died in somewhat mysterious circumstances, falling out of an upper-floor window. The rumor was that he committed suicide on being advised by his doctor of the necessity to follow a diet.[310]

## ...Revolution

⚜ The storming of the Bastille on July 14, 1789, a flashpoint in the French Revolution and widely regarded as an emblem of the abuses of the French monarchy, was essentially a symbolic act. At the time, there were only seven prisoners held there, mainly old men annoyed by the disturbance. The storming of the Bastille is celebrated to this day in France on July 14 with fireworks and a national holiday, known as Bastille Day.[311]

⚜ The French Revolutionary Calendar was a bizarre experiment in timekeeping introduced by the Revolutionary government for twelve years from 1793 to 1805, before it was abandoned. The principal aim of the Calendar was to decimalize and remove all trace of religion from timekeeping. Thus time started from the date of the foundation of the French Republic (September 22, 1792), the twelve months had their traditional names replaced with "poetic" French equivalents evoking the weather around Paris, and saints' days were replaced with patriotic days dedicated to French flora and fauna, crops, and proletarian tools. French citizens of the new Republic found themselves celebrating the day of the Plough, Grub-Hoe, Cauliflower, Beeswax, and Truffle. Each day in the Calendar was divided into ten hours and each hour into one hundred decimal minutes. The calendar ran from autumn to autumn. Clocks were made to keep time by the Calendar, but somehow it never caught on.

### Months of the Revolutionary Calendar

- Autumn:
  - Vendémiaire (month of the wine harvest), September/October
  - Brumaire (month of fog), October/November
  - Frimaire (month of frost), November/December
- Winter:
  - Nivôse (month of snow), December/January
  - Pluviôse (month of rain), January/February
  - Ventôse (month of wind), February/March
- Spring:
  - Germinal (month of germination), March/April
  - Floréal (month of flowering), April/May
  - Prairial (month of meadows), May/June

- Summer:
  - Messidor (month of the harvest), June/July
  - Thermidor (month of heat), July/August
  - Fructidor (month of fruits), August/September

☙ Although now defunct, relics of the Revolutionary Calendar subsist in French nomenclature to this day, including in the names of varieties of French garlic and the famous dish lobster Thermidor. Zola's revolutionary novel *Germinal* (1885), which tells the story of a worker revolt, consciously alludes to the Republican spring month in its title.[312]

☙ The name commonly given to the Revolutionaries during the years of the French Revolution was the *sansculottes* ("without breeches"). To distinguish themselves from the French nobility who wore the silk knee breeches called *culottes*, sansculottes wore long trousers called *pantalons*, short-skirted coats called *carmagnoles*, red caps to symbolize liberty, and clogs (*sabots*).[313]

☙ Louis XVI's attempt to escape from Paris in 1791 ended at Varennes, in northeastern France. However, just before this, the authorities were alerted by the postmaster at the village of Sainte-Ménéhould, through which the King had passed. The postmaster allegedly recognized the image of the king from a banknote.[314]

☙ One of the most famous and immediately identifiable of French paintings is *La Liberté guidant le people* ("*Liberty leading the people*") by Eugène Delacroix (1798–1863). Painted to commemorate the July Revolution in France that installed Louis-Philippe as a constitutional monarch in 1830 (also known as the Second French Revolution), the painting features the naked-breasted figure of Liberty leading a ragtag mob of scruffy French citizens to victory over oppression. Rising from a tangle of mangled corpses, Liberty herself combines elements of the symbolic personification of abstract ideals with those of a rough peasant woman. Her features are nobly chiseled, and she wears a Phrygian cap (the symbol of a freed slave in antiquity). But she also holds a bayonetted gun and—most shockingly of all—reveals the "vulgar" armpit hair that was banned from high art of the period. The painting was too inflammatory for Louis-Philippe and was not bought by the Royal Household; instead, it was purchased by the French Ministry of the Interior and hung in the Luxembourg Gallery. However, it was soon removed as too controversial, and spent the next few decades hidden from view, at one point in the attic of Delacroix's aunt. It was finally installed in the Louvre in 1874, where it quickly became one of the star attractions, second only to the *Mona Lisa*. In late 2012, the painting was removed to the new Louvre outpost in the grim northern French mining town of Lens. The move was hailed by some as a welcome transfer of the painting to a setting in keeping with its revolutionary worker spirit. Others have been more skeptical, deploring the loss from the French capital of one of its most iconic works of art. The painting was vandalized in 2013 by a twenty-eight-year-old woman, but almost immediately restored.[315]

## ...Rude

⚜ The French are famous for their rudeness, and indeed regularly top some travelers' polls for *impolitesse* in almost

| The Top Ten Countries for Rudeness in the 2012 Skycanner Poll[316] | |
|---|---|
| Nationality | Percentage of votes |
| French | 19.29 |
| Russian | 16.56 |
| British | 10.43 |
| German | 9.93 |
| Chinese | 4.3 |
| American | 3.39 |
| Spanish | 3.15 |
| Italian | 2.24 |
| Polish | 2.24 |
| Turkish | 2.15 |

every sector of public life. For example, a 2012 Skycanner survey reported by *Forbes* found that travelers voted the French the rudest country to visitors, followed by the Russians. (In defense of the French, it should be pointed out that most foreign visitors to France are limited to Paris, and do not experience the French outside the capital city.)

👑 When the makers of the BBC series of *The Mr Men* announced that Mr. Rude was to have a French accent, a spokesperson for the French ambassador to London stated that the new Mr. Rude "won't improve Anglo-French relations."[317]

👑 The French were not always celebrated for their rudeness, but rather the opposite in the time of the French monarchy: a highly civilized society with strict rules of politeness and decorum. It was the Revolution which first ushered in an era of *antipolitesse* as a form of rebellion against hierarchy. "Rudeness is a form of resistance to oppression," wrote the fanatical Jacobin Louis Antoine de Saint-Just. The polite *vous* form of address was abolished, along with titles: everybody was merely a "citizen" (*citoyen*), as was amply demonstrated by the trial of Marie-Antoinette.[318]

# S Is for...

### ...Salade niçoise

♛ The proper ingredients for the famous French dish salade niçoise are the subject of hot debate. The dish originated in the Provençal town of Nice, after which it is named. Traditionally, it contains a mixture of vegetables (tomatoes, peppers, red onions), olives, hard-boiled eggs, and anchovies. Purists insist that the vegetables should be raw, and the tomatoes salted three times. Cooked vegetables, rice, potatoes, and string beans are all considered Parisian abominations. Tuna is not—contrary to popular belief—an essential, and was not included in the nineteenth century because it was too expensive. Salade niçoise is traditionally accompanied by a Provençal rosé or light white wine.

---

### Salade Niçoise

Serves 4
**Ingredients**
  2 eggs
  1 small cucumber
  6 tomatoes (must be fresh, and preferably of the Saint
    Pierre variety)

3½ ounces of fresh fava beans
1 green pepper
3 small onions
1 clove garlic
10 anchovy fillets in oil
1 can of tuna in natural spring water
Olive oil
White wine vinegar
5 basil leaves
24 small black olives
Salt
Black pepper

## Method

1. Hard-boil the eggs. Peel the cucumber and cut into rounds, salt and let drain. Cut the tomatoes into rounds, salt and let drain. Shell the eggs.

2. Peel the beans. Wash the green pepper, cut in two, remove the seeds, and cut the skin into strips. Peel and chop the onions. Peel the clove of garlic. Remove excess oil from the anchovies and roll them into rounds.

3. Make up a vinaigrette with 5 tablespoons of oil and 2 tablespoons of vinegar. Season. Tear the basil leaves.

4. Rub the sides of a salad bowl with the garlic. Add the cucumbers, tomatoes, onions, beans, and pepper.

5. Add the vinaigrette and basil. Mix well.

6. Add a garnish of the eggs cut into rounds, olives, rolled anchovy fillets, and mashed tuna. Serve cold.

   *Et voilà!*

## ...School

&#9734; Until the mid-twentieth century in France, naughty school pupils were traditionally made to stand in the corner of the classroom sporting a paper hat with ass's ears on it. The dreaded *bonnet d'âne* sat perched on the teacher's desk, waiting for its next victim, until the early years of the twentieth century. A child who had to wear the *bonnet d'âne* also frequently had to wear a placard with the word *ÂNE* on it.

&#9734; The English equivalent of the *bonnet d'âne* was the "dunce's cap," a large paper cone with the letter *D* on it. The word *dunce* is said to have been coined as a derogatory term for the followers of the thirteenth-century philosopher Duns Scotus, although its use in the context of school discipline was first recorded in 1840, in Charles Dickens's novel *The Old Curiosity Shop*. Nowadays, the *bonnet d'âne* and dunce's cap have both thankfully disappeared into the more obscure annals of pedagogical history.[319]

&#9734; French school cafeterias are required by law to serve an entrée, main course, dessert, and *produit laitier* ("dairy product"), usually yogurt or cheese. The minimum time for a sitting is 30 minutes.[320]

&#9734; Unlimited self-service ketchup has been banned in French school cafeterias since 2011, as an "incarnation of Americanism." Ketchup can be served in limited cases, for example, with fries, which may only be served in one of five meals.[321]

&#9734; Ninety-six percent of schools in France have condom vending machines.[322]

# ...Sex

꙳ During the late sixteenth and seventeenth centuries in France, male impotence was considered a crime, as well as legal grounds for divorce. Men accused of impotence by their wives were required to demonstrate evidence to the contrary, by "standing to attention" and then ejaculating before an "expert panel" of clergymen and physicians. Not surprising, many gentlemen failed this audition. There was, however, a second chance. Should one wilt under scrutiny, one could request a "Trial by Congress," which entailed husband and wife performing sex before the judges. The practice was declared obscene and banned in 1677.[323]

꙳ France was the first country to legalize same-sex sexual activity, in 1791.[324]

꙳ In France brothels, known as the *maisons closes* ("closed houses"), were perfectly legal until they were abolished in 1946. The first of these started appearing in the 1820s. They were policed by some sensible regulations: they had to be discreet, with no obviously open windows, could not be set up on main boulevards, or within a hundred meters of a church or a school. Paris's bordellos soon became sensationally popular, frequented by film stars and heads of state. Their names were legendary: Le Chabanais, Le Sphinx, Chez Suzy, and The One Two Two. During World War II, they ran a roaring trade, servicing the German occupiers—until their closure in 1946, after the Armistice.[325]

꙳ The English playboy King Edward VII ("Bertie") was a great connoisseur of the French arts of love. His favorite brothel in Paris was Le Chabanais, established in 1878 by a certain Madame Kelly. The king's coat of arms was to be found over one of the beds, and there was also a magnificent tub and coordinated bidet in the shape of an enormous swan made of red copper, which Edward liked to fill with Champagne. The tub was eventually sold to the artist Salvador Dalí. The heavily overweight king also had a special chair made for him by a top French cabinetmaker, which allowed for easy access for oral and other types of sex with multiple participants.[326]

👑 French female writers have long been famous for their free views on morals and monogamy. The most notorious of them was probably the American-French-Cuban writer and diarist Anaïs Nin (1903–1977). Born and raised in France, Nin moved to America when war broke out in Europe in 1939. In 1923 she married her first husband, Hugh Guiler, a banker who lived in New York. However, in 1947, at the age of forty-four, she met the actor Rupert Pole—who was to move to California—in a Manhattan elevator, and secretly married him without Guiler's knowledge. She also had numerous affairs with a host of writers and artists, including the American writer Henry Miller. Nin referred to her simultaneous marriages as a "bicoastal trapeze." Her life was so complicated that she had two sets of checkbooks (one in the name of Mrs. Guiler for New York, and the other in the name of Mrs. Pole for Los Angeles). She kept a "lie box" in which she wrote down all the lies she had to make up, in order to remember them. She was so successful in her ruse that when she died in the 1970s, there were two separate obituaries for her: one in the New York newspapers, and one in those of Los Angeles. Nin is most famous for her diaries, in which she charted her many-faceted sex life and experiences. She was a devout follower of the Austrian psychoanalyst Otto Rank, who criticized Freud for failing to take account of female sexuality in his writings. In later life, she became a feminist icon.[327]

※ More than 75 percent of the slang English language phrases containing the word "French" are connected with sex. They include: French letter (condom), French maid, French pox or French disease (syphilis), French kissing, and the gay term Frenching (fellatio). Interestingly, many of these phrases are reversed the other way: a French slang term for condom is *capote anglaise* ("English hood"), and syphilis was referred to as *la maladie anglaise*.[328]

※ One of the first women to analyze and write about the phenomenon of female frigidity was, ironically, French. Princess Marie Bonaparte—whose great-granduncle was Napoleon— did not find sexual satisfaction in the arms of her husband, Prince George of Greece. This was perhaps not surprising, as he was a latent homosexual. However, she found no satisfaction in the arms of the prime minister of France either, or her husband's aide-de-camp, or numerous other lovers. She therefore set her theories of anatomical frigidity to the test by taking 243 women and measuring the distance between their clitoris and vagina, publishing the results in a 1924 medical and surgical issue of *Bruxelles-Médical*. Those women with a distance of 1 inch or more (21 percent) were, the princess stated, *téléclitoridiennes*—or "females of the distant clitoris"—and would be incapable of experiencing orgasm from penetrative sex alone. Those with a distance of less than an inch (69 percent) would be able to do so. Luckiest of all, she noted, however, were mares and cows, the clitorises of which were located "right on the border of the genital orifice." The princess also consulted

Sigmund Freud about her sexual issues, and it is to her that the psychoanalyst is said to have made his famous remark: "The great question that has never been answered and which I have not yet been able to answer, despite my thirty years of research into the feminine soul, is 'What does a woman want?' "[329]

♕ *Story of O* (*Histoire d'O*) is an erotic novel by a woman published under the pen name Pauline Réage, which caused a storm upon its publication in 1954. It is a tale of female submission in which O, a beautiful Parisian fashion photographer, is spirited off to a castle where she is made to serve the desires of an elite male sect. In the course of the story she willingly experiences blindfolding, chaining, whipping, branding, and labial piercing with the signature of her dominant English master, Sir Stephen. *Story of O* won the French literary prize *Les Deux Magots* on publication, but was subsequently investigated by the Paris vice squad. While "Pauline Réage" was always known to be a pseudonym, the true identity of the author of *Story of O* remained hidden for forty years after its publication. It was finally revealed that she was most probably Anne Cécile Desclos (1907–1998), an employee of French publishers Gallimard, who also wrote under the pen name of Dominique Aury. The book provoked feminist outrage (American college campus students burned copies in the 1980s), and many words in it have entered the terminology of the sadomasochist subculture.[330]

♕ France's most famous living dominatrix is a petite old lady called Catherine Robbe-Grillet, who was the mistress of the late French writer and notorious sadist Alain Robbe-Grillet. Now in her eighties, Madame Grillet lives in a château in Normandy with her lover and "slave," fifty-one-year-old Beverly Charpentier. The couple is at the head of a secret society of genteel female sadists, who include an actress with the *Comédie Française* and a well-known classical music critic. Unbeknown to their husbands and children, the women in the clique regularly get together for midnight whippings by the Seine, lit by passing riverboats, or for *La Chasse* ("The Hunt"), typically in a private Parisian park after dusk.[331]

☙ Despite their rich inheritance of erotic literature, the French seem to be less interested in reading about sex than other countries. At a symposium in London in 2009, Wikipedia founder Jimmy Wales revealed that sex was among the most popular article topics on Wikipedia in every language, except for French and Spanish. There was speculation, at the time, that this was possibly because the French and Spanish were actually having sex.[332]

## ...Snails

☙ The French consume more than 22 pounds of snails per second: that is, 15,000 tons of snails per year (mainly at Christmas, as snails are considered the ultimate festive food).[333]

☙ Every region in France has a different word for its local gastropod: *cagouilles* in Saintonge, *carago* in Provence, *carnar* in Lorraine, *schnacka* in Alsace, *lumas* in Poitou, and *cantaleu* in Nice.

☙ The classic French dish *escargots de Bourgogne* is supposed to have been invented by the great French chef Marie-Antoine Carême (1784–1833), for a dinner in honor of the tsar of Russia. The name of the dish, however, refers to the style of presenting the snails—smothered in garlic butter—and not to the fact of the snails coming from Burgundy. Native Burgundy snails are virtually extinct these days, so the snails in the average Parisian restaurant dish of *escargots de Bourgogne* will typically have come in frozen form, from eastern Europe.[334]

 ⚜ All snails caught in the wild have to be "purged" of any toxins they may have consumed and absorbed before they're fit for consumption. This is generally accomplished by keeping them in an airy box for a week or two, and feeding them only the freshest lettuce. Sometimes something colorful is used, so that it can be seen working through their system: the British chef Gordon Ramsay, for example, recommends feeding snails carrots during purging. The rather more heartless French technique is to shut the snails up and effectively starve them in a box for 2 weeks, with salt, a splash of vinegar, and a pinch of flour. There are various recommendations for cooking snails but death by boiling is the most popular.[335]

⚜ It is illegal to transport snails by French high-speed train (TGV), unless they have a ticket. A Frenchman was fined in 2008 for attempting to do just this, on the basis that any domestic animal on a train is required to have a ticket. The state-owned French company, SNCF, ended up waiving the fine.[336]

# T Is for...

## ...Tart

༺ France's most famous apple tart, *tarte tatin*, is said to have been invented by mistake. In the 1880s one of the Tatin sisters, who kept a modest inn in the town of Lamotte-Beuvron (Loir-et-Cher), put an apple tart in the oven and forgot to add the pastry topping. The singed, crispy confection that resulted subsequently became a house special, and was elevated to the heights of the best restaurants when the famous French food critic Curnonsky published the recipe.

Louis Vaudable, the owner of the Parisian restaurant Maxim's, who helped make *tarte tatin* a household name, gives an account of his "discovery" of the amazing new tart in his autobiography:

"I used to hunt around Lamotte-Beuvron in my youth, and had discovered in a very small hotel run by elderly ladies a marvelous dessert listed on the menu under 'tarte solognote.' I questioned the kitchen staff about its recipe, but was sternly rebuffed. Undaunted, I got myself hired as a gardener. Three days later, I was fired when it became clear that I could hardly plant a cabbage. But I had the recipe, and it became 'the tart of the Tatin sisters.'"[337]

# Easy Tarte Tatin

Recipes for *tarte tatin* range from the basic to fiendishly complex. Here is the simplest home version, adapted from a genuine French recipe.

Serves 6

**Ingredients**

   3 ½ ounces sugar

   2 ounces butter

   6 medium cooking apples

   juice of ½ lemon

   Cinnamon

   9 ounces of ready-prepared or homemade puff pastry.

**Method**

Cut the butter into pieces and place in an ovenproof/stovetop dish—ideally a Le Creuset *tarte tatin* mold—with the sugar. Cook on a gentle flame for at least 10 minutes with the lemon juice and cinnamon, or until it forms a caramelized consistency.

Peel, core, and cut the apples in half horizontally. Place in the dish. Cover with the rolled-out puff pastry.

Cook in the oven for 25 minutes at 410°F. Allow to cool before tipping out of the dish.

Serve warm (NEVER hot), with vanilla ice cream or *crème fraîche* (a traditional French soured cream).

Accompany with a sweet white dessert wine: Alsace, Pinot Gris, or Jurançon.

## …Toilet

🔱 Foreign visitors to Paris have traditionally quailed at the thought of having to face a "squat toilet," the hole in the ground that used to be the staple of Parisian bistros. But luckily, the squat toilet—variously labeled the French, Turkish, Greek, Bulgarian, Arabic, Chinese, Japanese, Korean, Iranian, Indian, or natural-position toilet—is being phased out in Paris, and is mainly to be encountered nowadays in rural areas or in highway rest stops.

🔱 Visitors to Paris will inevitably at some point encounter the rather ferocious female attendants in the public lavatories, known to the French as "Madame Pipi." They are unlikely to be aware, however, that these rather fierce ladies have a very distinguished pedigree. Their ranks have included the likes of the actress Marguerite Weimer, or "Mademoiselle George," mistress of Napoleon III and the tsar of Russia, who fell upon hard times and winded up her days doling out the toilet paper. There is even a professional qualification for a Madame Pipi offered in the city of Strasbourg, which includes training in detecting viruses, microbes, moss, and signs of mold, appropriate cleaning techniques, and how to deal with the amorous advances of clients.[338]

# U Is for...

## ...UFOs

A law of the French town of Châteauneuf-du-Pape bans UFOs or flying saucers from taking off, flying over, or landing on the town. The law dates from 1954, when the good burghers of the town became panicked by rumors of UFOs in the vicinity. In order to calm the population, the mayor introduced the law banning UFOs from flying over or landing on the town. More recently, a mayor of Châteauneuf refused to repeal the law, considering it part of the town's historical legacy.[339]

# V Is for...

## ...van Gogh

An unknown during his lifetime, the Dutch artist Vincent van Gogh painted most of his masterpieces in France (in the southern city of Arles and in Auvers-sur-Oise, outside of Paris). The intense Mediterranean light in the region of Arles was a major source of his inspiration, and it is after his stay in this city that he developed the palette of vivid yellows and greens for which his paintings became famous. Unfortunately, van Gogh's behavior became more and more peculiar. After a spat with the painter Gauguin in December 1888, for example, he went for him with a razor, and then (possibly in remorse) hacked off part of his own ear, delivering it personally to the local brothel before passing out on his blood-soaked bed. The next few years were spent in asylums, where many of his masterpieces were painted, in between bouts of craziness when the artist would poison himself by drinking his paints or his thinners. On June 27, 1890, van Gogh shot himself and died two days later, at the age of thirty-three. He was buried in a coffin smothered in yellow flowers, including his favorite, sunflowers. While only one of van Gogh's paintings sold in his lifetime, within a century of his death his *Portrait of Dr. Gachet* became the (then) world's most expensive painting, when it was sold in 1990 for $82.5 million. The only house in which he lived that remains intact is the Maison van Gogh at Auvers-sur-Oise, where his room—the cheapest lodging room in the establishment in 1890—can still be visited.[340]

The world's longest-living person, the French woman Jeanne Calment (1875–1997) lived all her long life in Arles and recalled van Gogh as "dirty, badly dressed, and disagreeable." In 1888, van Gogh allegedly came to a shop owned by Calment's uncle to buy paints. Calment was twelve or thirteen at the time and, according to her *New York Times* obituary, said van Gogh was "very ugly, ungracious, and impolite."[341]

[See separate entry for Jeanne Calment under subject heading *Femme.*]

# W Is for...

## ...War

♕ During World War I, government officials began creating a "fake Paris," a mock city on the outskirts of the real Paris, to throw German bombers off the scent. The plans for the sham city—which in the end was never built—were revealed in the *Illustrated London News* after the war, on November 6, 1920. There were to be sham streets lined with electric lights, sham rail stations, even sham industrial buildings. The city was also designed to have confusing lights and displays, so as to disorient German pilots into bombing and destroying it, rather than the real city.[342]

♕ During World War II, when France was occupied, the French cut the cables on the elevator in the Eiffel Tower, so that German soldiers had to climb to the top to hoist the swastika. When he visited the city, Hitler chose to opt out of the 1,500-step climb and remain with his feet firmly on the ground.[343]

♕ During World War II, the Grand Mosque of Paris helped Jews escape Nazi persecution by giving them Muslim IDs. Si Kaddour Benghabit, the rector of the Grand Mosque of Paris until 1954, smuggled hundreds of Jews and Resistance fighters into hiding in the vaulted caverns beneath the Mosque, while he took Nazi officers on tours of the buildings above. The

Grand Paris Mosque stands to this day in the 5th arrondissement, and houses one of the most beautiful open-air cafés in the city, which operates until midnight for a contemplative tea beneath the stars. The historically overlooked story of Si Kaddour Benghabit was the subject of a French film released in 2011, *Les Hommes Libres* (*Free Men*).[344]

꙳ When the Germans invaded Paris during the Second World War, the priceless art treasures of the Louvre were transported in secret to châteaux across France, where they were hidden by the wealthy owners until the end of the war.

꙳ Natzweiler-Struthof, located 31 miles southwest of Strasbourg, was the only concentration camp established by the Nazis on French soil.[345]

꙳ In 1944, as the Allies approached Paris, Hitler ordered Dietrich von Choltitz, the military governor of Paris, to demolish the Eiffel Tower. The general refused.[346]

## ...Wine

꙳ The French are the world's second-biggest wine producers, after Italy. They are the third-biggest wine consumers, at 44 liters per head per year. The number one world wine consumer is the Vatican City State, which downs an impressive 74 liters per head annually (presumably to be attributed to communion wine). Second comes the minuscule Principality of Andorra, whose inhabitants drink an average of 46 liters a year per head.[347]

꙳ The key point to bear in mind when deciphering French wine labels is that in France, the starting point for wine is the geographic area in which the wine is produced, or its *terroir*, and *not* the grape variety, as in New World wines. Foreigners can take heart from the fact that 72 percent of the adult population of France has difficulty understanding French wine labels.

💧 The average Frenchman drinks about a bottle of wine a week, six times more than the average American.[348]

💧 In 1984 in the French village of Vinsobres (literally, "sober wines"), in the Drôme, the local mayor banned the consumption of whiskey during the annual fair for the local Côtes-du-Rhone. The penalty was to be forced to consume a round of red wine. The stated justification was that "It is the consumption of alcohol which is dangerous, not wine."[349]

💧 The world's biggest market for Bordeaux wines today is China. In the past five years, more than twenty Bordeaux châteaux have been bought by the Chinese.[350]

💧 In 1971, the astronauts of NASA's *Apollo 15* moon mission named one of the lunar craters they found "St. George," in honor of the bottle of Nuits St. George consumed in Jules Verne's science fiction epic *From the Earth to the Moon* (1865):

"And lastly, to crown the repast, Ardan had brought out a fine bottle of Nuits, which was found 'by chance' in the provision box. The three friends drank to the union of the earth and her satellite."[351]

💧 The most expensive bottle of wine sold at retail was a limited edition Balthazar—a massive 12-liter bottle of Châteaux Margaux 2009. Produced in the Médoc to the north of Bordeaux, it went on sale in Dubai in 2013 for an eye-popping $195,000.[352]

💧 Contrary to the popular image of the Frenchman swilling red wine by the bottleful, in a recent polling of French drinking habits, red wine came a surprising third in the list, after Champagne and beer. The full results of the study, which was published in March 2014 and showed what percentage of those questioned had drunk specific beverages in the past twelve months, were as follows:

1. Champagne—71%
2. Beer—62%
3. Red wine—61%
4. Rosé—56%
5. Cider—55%
6. Dry white wine—50%
7. Kir—40%
8. Sparkling white wines and *crémants*—39%
9. Rum—37%
10. White spirits—34%
11. Whisky, bourbon—34%
12. Alcoholic cocktails—32%
13. Sweet wines—29%
14. Pastis—28%
15. Porto—28%

Sondage Baromètre Promise Consulting, Inc/
Le HuffPost

The Judgment of Paris is the name given to an infamous wine-tasting event that oc-curred in Paris in 1976, when Californian wines were pitted against native French vin-tages in a blind tasting by French experts that included leading wine writers and top chefs. The result—a great shock and humiliation for the French—was that, when the marks were tallied, wines from the Napa Valley came first in both the red and white categories. The lone reporter who covered the event was blacklisted for reporting it.[353]

### A guide to French wineglasses

While there are technically as many shapes of wineglass in France as of wine itself, things have simplified greatly in recent years just because it becomes too expensive and complicated to have more than half a dozen variations. The glasses most commonly to be found are: (1) the standard "red" glass traditionally used for Bordeaux, (2) the smaller and slightly taller glass for white, (3) the balloon glass traditionally used to capture the heady aroma of Burgundy wines, and (4) the Champagne flute. Don't expect to come across the massive wineglasses to be found in British and American restaurants, however. The standard glass of wine in the typical French bistro is 142 ml, compared to the "standard" British glass of 175 ml, or the vast "large" glass (250 ml), and the American standard of 240 ml.

♕ While the French approach to naming wines is generally conservative, some trendy new appellations—along the lines of the witty names devised by the U.S. wine label Charles Smith Wines—have begun to crop up. Recent examples include:

- *You fuck my wine?!*: A *vin de table* or "table wine" based on the red Jurançon (*Jurançon noir*) grape variety, produced by the otherwise very serious domain of Mas del Périé.
- *Ceci n'est pas un banane* ("This is not a banana"): a Beaujolais produced by the Lilian Bauchet vineyard

that plays on the frequent comparison to bananas of the aroma released by Beaujolais Nouveau.

- *Tout bu, or not tout bu*: Literally "To drink all or not to drink all," a table wine with a grandly Shakespearean pun on "To be or not to be," produced by the equally philosophically named Domaine du Possible in the Languedoc-Roussillon.

- *fucks@rkozy.com*: A limited edition and politically incorrect series of three thousand bottles produced in the run-up to the 2012 French presidential election by a small Beaujolais vineyard L'Astrolabe. The label—featuring the former president being squashed beneath the weight of an enormous barrel—was designed by Rénald Luzier ("Luz"), a cartoonist on the satirical magazine *Charlie Hebdo*. Luz narrowly missed being shot and killed in the massacre of 2015 because he turned up to the office late for work, arriving just in time to see the perpetrators fleeing.[354]

Other intriguing French wine names include Elephant on a Tightrope (from Vin de Pays d'Oc), Arrogant Frog and Frog's Piss, Vin de Merde (Languedoc-Roussillon), and the bestselling Fat Bastard (selling four hundred thousand cases in the United States alone, making it a marketing phenomenon).[355]

🍷 In the eighteenth century, "to have gone to Bordeaux" was slang for "to be drunk on red wine."[356]

## Rules for Serving French Wine

- Dry white wine, served very cold, is drunk with fish and seafood.

- Roast meat and poultry is served with light red wine (those of Bordeaux or the Loire region).

- Game and highly seasoned dishes pair with a rich Burgundy.

- Syrupy sweet white wines (such as Jurançon) are drunk with foie gras and some desserts.

- Champagne can go with anything, except for red meat. Most often, it serves as an apéritif before a meal begins.

- Rosé wine is for summer lunches and intimate dinners for two.

- Salads and crudités are not generally paired with wine (except for a salade niçoise, in summer, which goes well with rosé).

- During the course of a meal, lighter wines are served first, followed by heavier wines.

- Exceptionally, some dishes are not traditionally accompanied by wine: examples include mussels (usually served with beer), and crêpes (traditionally served with apple cider from Brittany).[357]

# X, Y, & Z Are for...

## ...The X-Files

♛ Officially the lowest-rated TV series by the French, along with *The Simpsons* and *Beverly Hills 90210*. The most popular TV series in France was voted as the American series *Criminal Minds*, followed by the (also American) *The Mentalist* and *NCIS*—revealing a decided penchant for U.S. cop flicks on the part of the French viewing public.[358]

## ...Marguerite Yourcenar

♛ Marguerite Yourcenar (1903–1987) was a Belgian-French novelist who became the first woman to be elected to the elite French language policing institution, the Académie Française, in 1980. Her most famous work—*Mémoires d'Hadrian*—was a fictional autobiographical account of the famous Roman emperor, and was published in 1951. She also translated Virginia Woolf's novel *The Waves* into French. Inclined toward bisexuality, Yourcenar lived with her companion Grace Frick in Maine until Frick's death in 1979. Rumor had it that, when she was elected the first female member of the Académie Française, the signs on the toilets were altered from *Messieurs* to *Messieurs/ Marguerite Yourcenar*.[359]

# ...Zinedine Zidane

♛ The former French soccer player and current coach for Real Madrid Castilla is affectionately known as "Zizou" to the French.

On September 26, 2012, a larger-than-life bronze statue of Zinedine Zidane head-butting Italian player Marco Materazzi was unveiled in the Pompidou Centre, Paris. The 16-foot statue by Algerian-born artist Adel Abdessemed, called *Headbutt*, recorded an event that occurred at the finals of the 2006 World Cup. Having faced opposition by the French directors of soccer associations, the statue was bought by the Qatari Museum Authority, which placed it on the Doha Corniche, Qatar. Causing again much criticism, it was taken down soon after, and moved into the Arab Museum of Modern Art in Doha.[360]

Zidane is the most penalized player in World Cup history. In twelve games over three tournaments, he received four yellow cards and two reds, including one for the infamous headbutt in the 2006 final. Only Brazil's Cafu has received as many cards, with six yellows across four tournaments.[361]

# Acknowledgments

This book could not have been written without the assistance of many conversations discussing the peculiarities and proclivities of the Gallic race, in the company of many friends (of all nationalities), over (several) bottles of wine. I am grateful to all of them! I am also thankful to the staff of the Bibliothèque Nationale and the British Library, in whose hallowed reading rooms I have spent many a happy hour looking up curious facts and figures. I am especially grateful also to Shelley Thevathasan, Eileen Bennett, Elizabeth Mockapetris, and Kelly Houle, for testing and commenting on some of the recipes. All errors, I hasten to add, are entirely my own.

Thanks are due to my fabulous agent, Andrew Lownie, to my brilliant editor, Emma Stein, and to all at Thomas Dunne/ St. Martin's Press.

Particular thanks to my mother, Sarah Das Gupta, husband Nikolaï, and sons Alek, Oscar, and Noah, for generally putting up with disruption to their lives of a more than trivial nature, while this book was being written.

# Notes

1   For details about absinthe, see Barnaby Conrad III, *Absinthe: History in a Bottle* (San Francisco: Chronicle Books, 1988); Phil Baker, *The Dedalus Book of Absinthe* (Sawtry, UK: Dedalus Limited, 2005); Cordelia Hebblethwaite, "Absinthe in France: Legalising the 'green fairy,'" *BBC News,* May 4, 2011.

2   Cited in Paul Owens and Paul Nathan, *The Little Green Book of Absinthe* (New York: Perigee/Penguin, 2010).

3   "France: Love in the Afternoon," *Time,* November 11, 1966, http://content.time.com/time/magazine/article/0,9171, 843018,00.html (subscription needed).

4   Paris Court of Appeal, February 13, 1986, cited in Paul de Vaublanc, *Plage interdite aux éléphants . . . : et autres bizarreries du droit!,* 2nd ed. (Levallois-Perret, France: Éditions Bréal, 2013), p. 58.

5   Saint-Léger-des-Prés, bylaw of April 1, 1991.

6   Town of Granville, bylaw of July 10, 2009.

7   Aude Seres, "Animaux de compagnie: la France championne d'Europe," *Le Figaro,* May 11, 2011, http://www.lefigaro.fr/actualite-france/2011/05/11/01016-20110511ARTFIG00749-animaux-de-compagnie-la-france-championne-d-europe.php.

8   Claude Pacheteau, "Les chiens préférés des Français en 2014," *Le Figaro,* March 13, 2014, http://www.lefigaro.fr/assurance

/2014/03/13/05005-20140313ARTFIG00290-les-chiens
-preferes-des-francais-en-2014.php.

9   Decision of the Court of Appeal of Rouen, dated November 22, 1978, cited in De Vaublanc, *Plage interdite aux éléphants*, p. 132.

10  Article 564 of the French Civil Code.

11  "Kangaroos run wild in France," *Sydney Morning Herald*, November 12, 2003, http://www.smh.com.au/articles/2003/11/12/1068329596677.html; Web site of the Mairie of Émancé, www.smh.com.au/articles/2003/11/12/1068329596677.html.

12  Robert Darnton, *The Great Cat Massacre: And Other Episodes in French Cultural History* (New York: Basic Books, 2009).

13  Jean-Michel Derex, *Les zoos de Paris: Histoire de la ménagerie du Jardin des Plantes, du Jardin d'acclimatation et du zoo de Vincennes* (Prahecq, France: Éditions Patrimoines & Médias, 2012).

14  Piers Letcher, *Eccentric France* (Chalfont St. Peter, UK: Bradt Travel Guides, 2003), p. 244.

15  Stephane Kirkland, *Paris Reborn: Napoléon III, Baron Haussmann, and the Quest to Build a Modern City* (New York: Picador, 2014).

16  Kenneth Frampton and Yukio Futagawa, *Modern Architecture, 1851–1945* (New York: Rizzoli, 1983), p. 106.

17  Yves Lucas, *Voyage dans les Marquises* (Paris: Au Même Titre, 2002).

18  Paris infographic at SmarterParis.com, http://www.smarterparis.com/infographic-paris-in-figures/.

19  Figures from ConsoGlobe/Planetoscope at Planetoscope.com.

20  Information Bulletin of French Artisan Boulangers.

21  French government circular; "Et le lauréat du Grand Prix de la meilleure baguette 2015 est . . . " *Next.paris.fr*, March 31, 2015.

22  "Cuisine. Le poulet rôti, plat préféré des Français," *Ouest-*

*France*, February 1, 2015, http://www.ouest-france.fr/econo mie/consommation/cuisine-le-poulet-roti-plat-prefere-des -francais-3156618.

23 Anthony Bourdain, "Solving the Mystery of French Steak," *New York Times*, July 12, 2000, http://partners.nytimes.com /library/dining/071200french-steak.html.

24 Helene Fouquet, "Last French Beret Maker Fights for Survival in Hollande Test," *Bloomberg Business*, February 18, 2014, http://www.bloomberg.com/news/articles/2014-02-17/last -beret-maker-in-france-fights-for-survival-in-hollande-test.

25 Ibid.

26 Ibid.

27 Piu Marie Eatwell, *They Eat Horses, Don't They? The Truth About the French* (New York: Thomas Dunne/St. Martin's Press, 2014).

28 Letcher, *Eccentric France*.

29 Adapted from Letcher, *Eccentric France*.

30 Jessica Kerwin Jenkins, *Encyclopedia of the Exquisite: An Anecdotal History of Elegant Delights* (New York: Nan A. Talese/ Doubleday, 2010).

31 Father Sebastiaan, *Mysteries of Paris* (New York: Bast Books, 2014), pp. 101–3; "Hell's Swells," *National Geographic*, August 2003, http://ngm.nationalgeographic.com/ngm/flashback /0308/.

32 City of Paris tourist guide for the grave of Philibert Asper.

33 Jon Henley, "In a secret Paris cavern, the real underground cinema," *Guardian*, September 8, 2004, http://www.theguar dian.com/world/2004/sep/08/filmnews.france; Sebastiaan, *Mysteries of Paris*, pp. 79–80.

34 Oscar Zaldaña Paredes, *Champagne: Facts, Mysteries, and Curiosities* (Bloomington, IN: Xlibris LLC, 2010), pp. 10–11.

35 Ian Parker, "He Knew He Was Right," *New Yorker*, October 16, 2006.

36 "Champagne: quelle est la marque préférée des Français?" *L'Union*, July 15, 2014, http://www.lunion.fr/accueil/cham pagne-quelle-est-la-marque-preferee-des-francais-ia0b0n-457050.

37 Ibid.

38 Paredes, *Champagne: Facts, Mysteries, and Curiosities*, p. 133.

39 Ibid.; Lise Ménalque, "Kate Moss et le sein à champagne," *Libération*, August 21, 2014, http://next.liberation.fr/mode/2014 /08/21/kate-moss-et-le-sein-a-champagne_1084254.

40 Roddy Button and Mike Oliver, *Wine—101 Truths, Myths and Legends* (Clacton on Sea, UK: Apex Publishing Ltd., 2013), Champagne No. 2.

41 Ibid., Closures & Openers No. 6.

42 Ibid.

43 J. Randy Taraborrelli, *The Secret Life of Marilyn Monroe* (London: Sidgwick & Jackson, 2009); Paredes, *Champagne: Facts, Mysteries, and Curiosities*, p. 134.

44 Button and Oliver, *Wine—101 Truths, Myths and Legends*, Champagne No. 8.

45 Names and liter equivalents taken from adorechampagne .com.

46 Button and Oliver, *Wine—101 Truths, Myths and Legends*, Champagne No. 4.

47 Per capita cheese consumption figures for France, the UK, and the US for 2010 (total per capita consumption) from the Canadian Dairy Information Centre, http://www.dairyinfo .gc.ca/index_e.php.

48 "Mont d'Or ou Vacherin Mont d'Or," androuet.com/liste -fromage/html.

49 "'World's smelliest cheese' named," *BBC News*, November 26, 2004, http://news.bbc.co.uk/2/hi/uk_news/england/beds/bucks /herts/4044703.stm.

50 *The Bonne Femme Cookbook, How to Serve a Cheese Course* . . .

*the French Way*, http://chezbonnefemme.com/how-to-make-it
-french/how-to-serve-a-cheese-course-the-french-way/.

51 Etude GFK, 2011.

52 *Le Grand Robert: Langue française*, s.v. "chef, n.m."

53 Patrick Rambourg, *Histoire de la cuisine et de la gastronomie françaises* (Paris: Éditions Perrin, 2010).

54 Eatwell, *They Eat Horses, Don't They?*; David Alliot et al., *La tortue d'Eschyle et autres morts stupides de l'Histoire* (Paris: Les Arènes, 2012), chap. 1 ("Trop gourmands").

55 Virginie Langerock, *La France, championne d'Europe des naissances*, French Office of Foreign and Diplomatic Affairs, March 2011.

56 *Code de l'action sociale et des familles*, Articles D215-7 and D215-8.

57 Anne Penketh, "Nutella not a girl's name, French court rules," *Guardian*, January 26, 2015, http://www.theguardian.com /world/2015/jan/26/french-couple-name-girl-nutella.

58 OECD key tables on health, tobacco consumption for 2008, http://www.oecd.org/; François Beck et al., *Premiers résultats du baromètre santé 2010: Evolutions récentes du tabagisme en France* (Saint Denis, France: Institut National de Prévention et d'Éducation Pour la Santé, January 28, 2010), p. 3, http:// www.inpes.sante.fr/30000/pdf/Evolutions-recentes-tabagisme -barometre-sante2010.pdf.

59 Eatwell, *They Eat Horses, Don't They?*

60 Ipsos, *Tabac et cinema*, June 1, 2012, https://www.ligue-cancer .net/presse/download/506.

61 Kenneth Davids, *Coffee: A Guide to Buying, Brewing, and Enjoying* (New York: St. Martin's Griffin, 2001).

62 Honoré de Balzac, "The Pleasures and Pains of Coffee," translated from the French by Robert Onopa, originally published in the *Michigan Quarterly Review* 35, no. 2 (Spring 1996), pp. 273–77.

63   David Kamp, "The Hacker and the Hack," *New York Times Sunday Book Review*, May 28, 2010.

64   List of Intangible Cultural Heritage, www.unesco.org.

65   Flora Bruyère, "La cuisine italienne: cuisine étrangère préférée des Français," *Mingle Trend*, March 31, 2011, http://mingle-trend.respondi.com/fr/cuisine-etrangere-preferee-des-francais/.

66   Doug Lansky, *The Titanic Awards* (New York: Perigee/Penguin, 2010).

67   Michelin Guide 2015.

68   "Recette signee DAVY," *Le Monde Cuisiner*, April 17, 2011.

69   Olivier Gaudant, *Petit traité des sauces* (Chambéry, France: Éditions Le Sureau, 2011).

70   *Larousse Gastronomique* (London: Hamlyn/Octopus, 1988).

71   Ibid.

72   Isabelle Marique and Albert Jorant, *The French Cuisine of Your Choice* (New York: Harper & Row, 1981).

73   Nichola Fletcher, *Sausage: A Country-by-Country Photographic Guide with Recipes* (London: Dorling Kindersley, 2012).

74   Charles Ranhofer, *The Epicurean* (New York, 1894).

75   Martin Hannan, *Harvey Wallbangers and Tam O'Shanters: A Book of Eponyms* (London: Metro Publishing/John Blake Publishing, 2011).

76   Victor Hirtzler, *The 1910 Hotel St. Francis Cook Book* (Sausalito, CA: Windgate Press, 1988).

77   Article 171 of the French Civil Code.

78   Bylaw of 2008, cited in De Vaublanc, *Plage interdite aux éléphants*, p. 77.

79   Terry Breverton, *Immortal Last Words: History's Most Memorable Dying Remarks, Deathbed Declarations and Final Farewells* (London: Quercus, 2010).

80   Rev. S. F. Smith, "Last Days of Eminent Men," *The Christian Review* 11 (1846).

81   Breverton, *Immortal Last Words*.

82    C. Bernard Ruffin, *Last Words: A Dictionary of Deathbed Quotations* (Jefferson, NC: McFarland, 2006); see also Eric Grounds, *The Bedside Book of Final Words* (Stroud, UK: Amberley Publishing, 2014).

83    Breverton, *Immortal Last Words.*

84    Grounds, *The Bedside Book of Final Words;* see also Alan Bisbort, *Famous Last Words: Apt Observations, Pleas, Curses, Benedictions, Sour Notes, Bons Mots, and Insights from People on the Brink of Departure* (Rohnert Park, CA: Pomegranate Communications, 2001).

85    Ibid.

86    Rev. S. F. Smith, "Last Days of Eminent Men."

87    Herbert Lockyer, *Last Words of Saints and Sinners: 700 Final Quotes from the Famous, the Infamous, and the Inspiring Figures of History* (Grand Rapids, MI: Kregel, 1969).

88    Grounds, *The Bedside Book of Final Words.*

89    Tracey Turner, *Dreadful Fates: What a Shocking Way to Go!* (London: A & C Black, 2010); see also Grounds, *The Bedside Book of Final Words.*

90    Grounds, *The Bedside Book of Final Words.*

91    Bisbort, *Famous Last Words.*

92    Ibid.

93    Ibid.

94    Michael Evans, *The Death of Kings: Royal Deaths in Medieval England* (London: Hambledon Continuum, 2007).

95    Lockyer, *Last Words of Saints and Sinners.*

96    Ibid.

97    Nigel Starck, *Life After Death: The Art of the Obituary* (Melbourne: Melbourne University Press, 2006).

98    Simon Critchley, *The Book of Dead Philosophers* (London: Granta Books, 2008).

99    *The Penny Cyclopaedia of the Society for the Diffusion of Useful Knowledge*, vol. 11 (London: Charles Knight & Co., 1838).

100  Anil Aggrawal, *Necrophilia: Forensic and Medico-legal Aspects* (Boca Raton, FL: CRC Press, 2011), pp. 4, 11–12; *Oxford English Dictionary*, s.v. "necrophilia"; Joseph G. Ramsey, "Guy Endore and the Ironies of Political Repression," *Minnesota Review*, no. 70 (2008), 141–51.

101  Vanessa R. Schwartz, *Modern France: A Very Short Introduction* (New York: Oxford University Press, 2011).

102  Cited in A. K. M. Adam and Samuel Tongue, eds., *Looking through a Glass Bible* (Leiden, Netherlands: Brill, 2013).

103  Caitlind L. Alexander, *14 Fun Facts about the Eiffel Tower* (LearningIsland.com, 2011).

104  Rose Collis, *Death and the City* (Brighton, UK: Hanover Press/Victorian Secrets Ltd., 2013).

105  Joseph Harriss, *The Tallest Tower: Eiffel and the Belle Epoque* (Bloomington, IN: Unlimited Publishing, 2004).

106  Ibid.; see also Serge Garde et al., *Guide du Paris des faits divers* (Paris: Le Cherche Midi, 2013).

107  Harriss, *The Tallest Tower.*

108  Ibid.

109  Aislinn Simpson, "Woman with objects fetish marries Eiffel Tower," *Telegraph*, June 4, 2008, http://www.telegraph.co.uk/news/newstopics/howaboutthat/2074301/Woman-with-objects-fetish-marries-Eiffel-Tower.html.

110  Patricia de Prelle et al., *Le Guide de l'Étiquette de du Savoir-Vivre* (Brussels: Editions Racine, 2001).

111  Ibid.

112  Ibid.

113  Boris Kachka, "Etiquette 101: France," *Condé Nast Traveler*, October 15, 2007.

114  De Prelle, *Le Guide de l'Étiquette de du Savoir-Vivre.*

115  Kachka, "Etiquette 101: France."

116  Lucie Létourneau and Fabio Pellegrino, *Recevoir et être reçu*

*(Savoir-vivre et etiquette t. 1)*, Kindle ed. (Montreal: Les Editions LaLucia, 2013).

117  De Prelle, *Le Guide de l'Étiquette de du Savoir-Vivre.*

118  Joan DeJean, *The Essence of Style: How the French Invented High Fashion, Fine Food, Chic Cafés, Style, Sophistication, and Glamour* (New York: Free Press, 2005).

119  Ibid.

120  For a detailed history of the Breton shirt, see Eatwell, *They Eat Horses, Don't They?*

121  *Oxford English Dictionary*, s.v. "denim"; Bill Marshall and Cristina Johnston, eds., *France and the Americas: Culture, Politics, and History* (Santa Barbara, CA: ABC-CLIO, 2005).

122  Bernard Andrieu, *Bronzage: Une petite histoire du soleil et de la peau* (Paris: CNRS Editions, 2008).

123  Amy Holman Edelman, *The Little Black Dress* (London: Aurum, 1998).

124  Debbie Millman, ed., *Brand Bible: The Complete Guide to Building, Designing, and Sustaining Brands* (Beverly, MA: Rockport, 2012).

125  Nigel Crawford, *Key Moments in Fashion* (New York: Sterling Publishing, 2001).

126  Michael Tonello, *Bringing Home the Birkin: my life in hot pursuit of the world's most coveted handbag* (New York: Harper-Collins, 2008); Luke Leitch, "How Jane's Birkin bag idea took off," *Telegraph*, July 26, 2015, http://www.telegraph.co .uk/fashion/people/how-jane-birkins-hermes-bag-idea-took -off/.

127  Lauren Milligan, "Louboutin Lover," *Vogue*, April 1, 2010.

128  Jean-Noël Kapferer and Vincent Bastien, *The Luxury Strategy: Break the Rules of Marketing to Build Luxury Brands*, 2nd ed. (London: Kogan Page Limited, 2012).

129  *People with Money*, February 2015.

130  Grégory Raymond, "Marques de lingerie féminine préférées des Français," *Baromètre Promise Consulting Inc./Le Huffington Post,* February 13, 2014.

131  Figures from ConsGlobe/Planetoscope at www.planetoscope .com.

132  Caroline Castets, "A la Une également—French paradox," *Le Nouvel Economiste,* April 27, 2011, http://www.lenouvelecono miste.fr/french-paradox-10031/; key figures for meals and turnover from McDonald's for the year 2011.

133  Lansky, *The Titanic Awards.*

134  Craig Glenday, ed., *Guinness World Records, 2015* (New York: Bantam Books/Random House, 2014); Craig R. Whitney, "Jeanne Calment, World's Elder, Dies at 122," *New York Times,* August 5, 1997, http://www.nytimes.com/1997/08/05/world /jeanne-calment-world-s-elder-dies-at-122.html.

135  L'ordonnance du préfet de police Dubois n°22 du 16 brumaire an IX (7 novembre 1800); circulars of 1892 and 1909 authorizing the wearing of trousers by women "if the woman holds in her hand the handle of a bicycle or reins of a horse"; AFP, "Le pantalon n'est plus interdit pour les Parisiennes," *Libération,* February 4, 2013.

136  Claire Duchen, *Women's Rights and Women's Lives in France, 1944–1968* (London: Routledge, 1994).

137  John Ardagh, *France Today* (London: Penguin, 1995), p. 331; "Croque-mort, sous-officier CRS . . . des métiers encore interdits aux femmes," *Planet.fr,* April 16, 2014, http://www.planet .fr/societe-croque-mort-sous-officier-crs-des-metiers-encore -interdits-aux-femmes.593173.29336.html.

138  Ibid.

139  Liz Sonneborn, *A to Z of American Women in the Performing Arts* (New York: Facts on File, 2002).

140  Michael Phillips, "Oscars: 'The Artist' wins best picture," *Chicago Tribune,* February 27, 2012, http://articles.chicagotribune

.com/2012-02-27/entertainment/chi-oscars-academy-awards
-main-20120223_1_actress-oscar-race-1982-s-sophie-s-choice
-meryl-streep-best-actress.

141  Eatwell, *They Eat Horses, Don't They?*

142  "Louis de Funès et Sophie Marceau, acteurs préférés des
Français," *L'Express,* March 28, 2015, http://www.lexpress.fr
/culture/cinema/louis-de-funes-et-sophie-marceau-acteurs
-preferes-des-francais_1665929.html.

143  Ibid.

144  Ibid.

145  Brian Clark, "Le Beverley Cinéma: Last porn theatre in Paris,"
*Vingt Paris,* January 2, 2012, http://www.vingtparis.com
/parigot/cest-lamour-last-porn-theatre-in-paris-is-more-than
-just-porn/; Web site of Beverley Cinema at www.le-beverley
.info.

146  Letcher, *Eccentric France.*

147  Nigel Groom, *The Perfume Handbook* (New York: Springer-
Science+Business Media, 1992).

148  Colin Jones, *The Cambridge Illustrated History of France* (Cambridge, UK: Cambridge University Press, 1994).

149  World Tourism Organization/Deutsche Welle, August 20, 2014.

150  "France," *The World Factbook, Central Intelligence Agency,* updated March 6, 2014, https://www.cia.gov/library/publications
/the-world-factbook/.

151  Ibid.

152  Ibid.

153  Study carried out for the *Huffington Post/Active Times,* February 2015, by advisers to UNESCO's World Heritage Com-
mittee.

154  "Shift Ranking of June 24: Countries with the most UNESCO
World Heritage Sites," *Deutsche Welle,* June 24, 2013, http://
www.dw.com/en/shift-ranking-of-june-24-countries-with-the
-most-unesco-world-heritage-sites/a-16902900.

155   "39: The number of French sites included on UNESCO's
      World Heritage List," *France Diplomatie*, French government
      diplomatic Web site, http://www.diplomatie.gouv.fr/en/french
      -foreign-policy/economic-diplomacy-foreign-trade/facts
      -about-france/one-figure-one-fact/article/39-the-number-
      of-french-sites.

156   Xavier de Jarcy et Vincent Remy, "Comment la France est de-
      venue moche," *Enquête Télérama*, February 13, 2010, http://
      www.les-sorgues-vertes.com/76+comment-la-france-est
      -devenue-moche-telerama.html.

157   "The Narrative of Numbers, Disneyland Paris in Figures,"
      Disneyland Paris, http://corporate.disneylandparis.com/about
      -our-company/the-narrative-of-numbers/index.xhtml.

158   *Le Grand Robert: Langue française,* s.v. "Marseillaise, la."

159   Lansky, *The Titanic Awards.*

160   World Health Organization Survey, July 2011.

161   Eatwell, *They Eat Horses, Don't They?*; Hildegard L. C. Tristram,
      *The Celtic Languages in Context* (Potsdam, Germany: Potsdam
      University Press, 2007).

162   Joseph Bamat, "Inside the Académie Française with Sir Mi-
      chael Edwards," *France 24,* http://webdoc.france24.com/inside
      -the-academie-francaise/.

163   Susie Dent, ed.. , *Brewer's Dictionary of Phrase and Fable,* 19th rev.
      ed. (London: Hodder Education, 2012); Jonathon Green, *Green's
      Dictionary of Slang* (London: Chambers Harrap, 2012), s.vv.
      "Frog" and "Froglander"; Eatwell, *They Eat Horses, Don't They?*

164   Jon Henley, "A short history of frog eating," *Guardian*, Au-
      gust 7, 2009, http://www.theguardian.com/lifeandstyle/2009
      /aug/07/frogs-legs-france-asia.

165   Ibid.

166   Elizabeth David, *French Provincial Cooking* (London: Michael
      Joseph, 1960).

167   Henley, "A short history of frog eating."

168 Sandra Altherr et al., "Canapés to Extinction: The International Trade in Frogs' Legs and Its Ecological Impact (report by Pro Wildlife, Defenders of Wildlife, and Animal Welfare Institute, Munich, Germany, and Washington, DC, 2011), http://www.defenders.org/sites/default/files/publications /canapes_to_extinction.pdf.

169 "Garlic," *France Agrinet, Le Magazine*.

170 *Le Grand Robert: Langue française,* s.v. "chandail, n.m."

171 LMJ International Limited; Andy Mukherjee, "South Korea's Mr Garlic strives for openness," *Bloomberg*, June 7, 2004; Matthieu Serrurier, "Economie et marché de l'ail," Centre Technique Interprofessionnel des Fruits et Légumes, March 16, 2011, www.ctifl.tr.

172 Françoise de Motteville, *Mémoires* (1648).

173 "Histoire de la galette des rois et de la fève," *L'Express Styles*, January 6, 2015, http://www.lexpress.fr/styles/saveurs/histoire -de-la-galette-des-rois-et-de-la-feve_1637819.html.

174 Graeme Donald, *Lies, Damned Lies and History* (Stroud, UK: The History Press, 2009).

175 Ibid.

176 Ibid.

177 Daniel Gerould, *Guillotine: Its Legend and Lore* (New York: Blast Books, 1992).

178 Ibid.

179 Ibid.

180 European Observatory for drugs and toxins report, as cited in TFI report, May 27, 2014.

181 Ernest L. Abel, *Marihuana: The First Twelve Thousand Years* (New York: Plenum Press, 1980), pp. 148–49.

182 Ibid.; *Oxford English Dictionary,* s.v. "assassin, n.," etymology.

183 Charles Baudelaire, *The Poem of Hashish*, translated by Aleister Crowley (1895). See https://www.erowid.org/culture/characters /baudelaire_charles/baudelaire_charles_poem1.shtml.

184  Alice B. Toklas, *The Alice B. Toklas Cook Book*, 2nd ed. (London: Serif, 1998).

185  "Haschich Fudge" [pp. 259–60] from *The Alice B. Toklas Cook Book* by Alice B. Toklas. Copyright 1954 by Alice B. Toklas. Copyright renewed 1982 by Edward M. Burns. Foreword copyright © 1984 by M. F. K. Fisher. Publisher's Note copyright © 1984 by Simon Michael Bessie. Reprinted by permission of HarperCollins Publishers.

186  See entries for individual words in *Oxford English Dictionary*; also Hannan, *Harvey Wallbangers and Tam O'Shanters*.

187  *Le Grand Robert: Langue française*, s.v. "poubelle, n.f."

188  Letcher, *Eccentric France*; P. A. Gowens et al., "Survival from accidental strangulation from a scarf resulting in laryngeal rupture and carotid artery stenosis: the 'Isadora Duncan syndrome,'" *Emergency Medicine Journal* 20, no. 4 (2003), http://emj.bmj.com/content/20/4/391.full.

189  Timothy R. Levine, ed., *Encyclopedia of Deception* (Los Angeles: Sage Publications, 2014), p. 30.

190  Linda Polon and Aileen Cantwell, *The Whole Earth Holiday Book* (Glenview, IL: Good Year Books/Scott, Foresman and Co., 1983).

191  Martin, "Les poissons sont de retour!" www.frenchmoments .eu, March 25, 2013,"

192  "Top 10 April Fool's hoaxes," *Telegraph*, April 1, 2009, http://www.telegraph.co.uk/news/newstopics/howaboutthat/5086490/Top-10-April-Fools-hoaxes.html.

193  Olivier Cabanel, "Avril, le mois du poisson," AgoraVox, March 31, 2015, http://www.agoravox.fr/culture-loisirs/etonnant/article/avril-le-mois-du-poisson-165525.

194  Sebastien Tronche, "Le poisson d'avril du député Poisson ne fait pas l'unanimité à l'UMP," *Le Lab Europe 1*, April 1, 2013, http://lelab.europe1.fr/le-poisson-d-avril-du-depute-jean

-frederic-poisson-pour-proteger-les-deputes-qui-portent-
un-nom-d-animal-aquatique-ne-fait-pas-l-unanimite-a-l-
ump-8152.

195 "Le Top 5 des poissons de ce 1er avril," *lalsace.fr*, April 1, 2014,
http://www.lalsace.fr/actualite/2014/04/01/le-top-5-des
-poissons-d-avril.

196 Hélène Delalex et al., *Louis XIV pour les nuls* (Paris: Éditions
First-Gründ, 2011).

197 *New York Times*, January 29, 1911.

198 Glenday, *Guinness World Records, 2015*.

199 Holly Watt and Claire Newell, "Hunt for £20m Easter egg
bought by 'A Stranger,'" *Telegraph*, April 12, 2014, http://
www.telegraph.co.uk/culture/art/art-news/10761685/Hunt
-for-20m-Easter-egg-bought-by-A-Stranger.html.

200 *Oxford English Dictionary*, s.v. "dauphin, n."; also *Le Grand
Robert: Langue française*, s.v. "dauphin, n.m."

201 Preston Russell, *Lights of Madness: In Search of Joan of Arc*
(Bloomington, IN: Xlibris, 2014).

202 HRH Princess Michael of Kent, *The Serpent and the Moon:
Two Rivals for the Love of a Renaissance King* (New York: Touch-
stone/Simon & Schuster, 2004).

203 Norman L. Cantor, *After We Die: The Life and Times of the
Human Cadaver* (Washington, DC: Georgetown University
Press, 2010), p. 55.

204 Will and Ariel Durant, *The Story of Civilization, vol. 7, The
Age of Reason Begins* (New York: Simon & Schuster, 1961),
chapter 13.

205 Norris McWhirter, *Guinness Book of World Records, 1986* (New
York: Bantam Books, 1985); Lewis Dean, "Queen Elizabeth II
longest reign: Monarch overtakes Queen Victoria record for time
on the throne," *International Business Times*, September 9, 2015,
http://www.ibtimes.co.uk/queen-elizabeth-ii-longest-reign

-monarch-overtakes-queen-victoria-record-time-throne
-1518925.

206  René Chartrand, *French Fortresses in North America, 1535–
1763: Québec, Montréal, Louisbourg and New Orleans* (Oxford,
UK: Osprey Publishing, 2005).

207  Eatwell, *They Eat Horses, Don't They?*

208  Delalex, *Louis XIV pour les nuls.*

209  Letcher, *Eccentric France.*

210  Michel Bernard Cartron, *Louis XIX, celui qui fut roi 20 minutes* (Versailles: Via Romana, 2010); McWhirter, *Guinness Book
of World Records,* 1986.

211  "Classic kiss shot sold at auction," *BBC News,* April 25, 2005,
http://news.bbc.co.uk/2/hi/entertainment/4481789.stm; Val
Williams, "Obituary: Robert Doisneau," *Independent,* April
2, 1994, http://www.independent.co.uk/news/people/obituary
-robert-doisneau-1367399.html.

212  "French, second-most-studied foreign language in Europe,"
*France Diplomatie,* October 2014, http://www.diplomatie.gouv
.fr/en/french-foreign-policy/economic-diplomacy-foreign
-trade/facts-about-france/one-figure-one-fact/article/french
-second-most-studied-foreign.

213  *The World Factbook, Central Intelligence Agency* for each of
these countries.

214  Jean-Benoît Nadeau and Julie Barlow, *The Story of French*
(London: Portico, 2010).

215  Ibid.

216  Francis Katamba, *English Words: Structure, History, Usage,*
2nd ed. (Abingdon, UK: Routledge, 2005).

217  "Why Mayday?" *Research Questions, National Maritime Museum, Cornwall,* http://www.nmmc.co.uk/index.php?/collect
ions/featured_questions/why_mayday; John Rousmaniere, *The
Annapolis Book of Seamanship,* 4th ed. (New York: Simon &
Schuster, 2014).

218 Max Cryer, *Curious English Words and Phrases: The truth behind the expressions we use* (Auckland, New Zealand: Exisle Publishing, 2012).

219 *Oxford English Dictionary*, s.v. "dandelion, n."; *Le Grand Robert: Langue française*, s.v. "pissenlit, n.m."

220 *Oxford English Dictionary*, s.v. "mortgage, n."

221 Robert A. Palmatier, *Speaking of Animals: A Dictionary of Animal Metaphors* (Westport, CT: Greenwood Press, 1995), p. 245.

222 Paul Anthony Jones, *Word Drops: A Sprinkling of Linguistic Curiosities*, Kindle ed. (London: Elliott & Thompson, 2015).

223 William E. Kruck, *Looking For Dr. Condom*, Publication of the American Dialect Society #66 (Tuscaloosa, AL: University of Alabama Press, 1981); Letcher, *Eccentric France.*

224 All word definitions in these sections from the *Oxford English Dictionary* and *Le Grand Robert: Langue française.*

225 "Game of Nobels: The top 10," *Wall Street Journal*, October 13, 2014; Ashley Kirk, "Nobel Prize winners," *Telegraph*, October 12, 2015, http://www.telegraph.co.uk/news/worldnews/northamerica/usa/11926364/Nobel-Prize-winners-Which-country-has-the-most-Nobel-laureates.html.

226 Robert T. Lambdin and Laura C. Lambdin, eds., *Encyclopedia of Medieval Literature* (London: Fitzroy Dearborn Publishers, 2000).

227 Noel L. Griese, "The Bible vs. Mao: A 'Best Guess' of the Top 25 Bestselling Books of All Time," *Publishing Perspectives*, September 7, 2010, http://publishingperspectives.com/2010/09/top-25-bestselling-books-of-all-time/.

228 "Toujours n 1 des best-sellers," *L'Express*, June 18, 2009.

229 Brian Taves, "Jules Verne's *Paris in the Twentieth Century*," *Science Fiction Studies* 24, no. 71, part 1 (March 1997).

230 Frances Perraudin, "Meet the Real James Bonds: Fast Cars, But No License to Kill," *Time*, September 23, 2010, http://newsfeed

.time.com/2010/09/23/meet-the-real-james-bonds-fast-cars
-but-no-license-to-kill/.

231   Charles Perrault, *Perrault's Fairy Tales* (Mineola, NY: Dover Publications, 1969); Margaret Early, *Sleeping Beauty* (New York: Harry N. Abrams, 1993); Philippe Seydoux, *Chateaux of the Val de Loire* (New York: Vendome Press, 1992).

232   Georges Perec, *Le grand palindrome*, Perec et Pitres, 2009.

233   Timothy T. Fullerton, *Triviata: A Compendium of Useless Information* (Outlet, 1975); report in *BBC Today*, October 3, 2014.

234   Translated from the French by C. K. Scott Moncrieff, 1922.

235   "The 10 Longest Novels Ever Written," *ShortList Magazine*, http://www.shortlist.com/entertainment/books/the-10 -longest-novels-ever-written.

236   Bisbort, *Famous Last Words*; Bill Hoffmann, "Mata Hari Heads Off—Femme Fatale's Skull Swiped from Museum," *New York Post*, July 14, 2000, http://nypost.com/2000/07/14/mata-hari -heads-off-femme-fatales-skull-swiped-from-museum/.

237   Data from French environmental marketing agency Planeto-scope/consoGlobe.

238   *Le Grand Robert: Langue française*, s.v. "merde, interj."

239   Ibid.

240   *Oxford English Dictionary*, "French toast, n."

241   Jim Chevallier, *August Zang and the French Croissant: How Viennoiserie Came to France* (Chez Jim, 2009); *Le Grand Robert: Langue française*, s.v. "croissant, n."

242   "Comment un garçon vacher, en Normandie, a inventé le 'Petit Suisse,'" Danone company Web site at www.danone.ch.

243   Chef Charles Oppman, *Accidental Chef: An Insider's View of Professional Cooking* (Bloomington, IN: AuthorHouse, 2011).

244   Sadie Whitelocks, "Is the French manicure actually American?" *Daily Mail*, April 15, 2013, http://www.dailymail.co.uk /femail/article-2309562/Is-French-manicure-actually

-AMERICAN-Hollywood-make-artist-claims-invented
-classic-white-tip-nude-nail-look.html.

245  Julia Child et al., *Mastering the Art of French Cooking* (London: Penguin, 2011); Geoffrey T. Hellman, "Tasting Menu—Diat," *New Yorker*, December 2, 1950.

246  International Horn Society information bulletin.

247  "Le Bouledogue Français: ses origines," *Club du Bouledogue Français*, http://www.cbf-asso.org/txt/bouledogue_origines.htm.

248  Sarah Rainey, "11 odd fast food facts: which president pioneered French fries?" *Telegraph*, November 5, 2015, http://www.telegraph.co.uk/foodanddrink/11369509/11-odd-fast-food-facts-which-president-launched-the-French-fry.html; Lawrence R. Schehr and Allen S. Weiss, eds., *French Food: On the Table, On the Page, and in French Culture* (Abingdon, UK: Routledge, 2001), p. 158; Natalia Sloam, "10 Things You Didn't Know About French Fries," *Daily Meal*, July 11, 2014, http://www.thedailymeal.com/10-things-you-didn-t-know-about-french-fries.

249  Sydney Beveridge, "Get your Country out of my Happy Meal!: Liberty cabbage, Freedom fries and other Product Renamings," *Mental Floss*, July 14, 2008, http://mentalfloss.com/article/19061/get-your-country-out-my-happy-meal-liberty-cabbage-freedom-fries-and-other-product.

250  Eatwell, *They Eat Horses, Don't They?*

251  *Le Grand Robert: Langue française.*

252  Jack Mingo, *How the Cadillac Got Its Fins: And Other Tales from the Annals of Business and Marketing* (New York: HarperCollins, 1995); Rik Riezebos et al., *Brand Management: A Theoretical and Practical Approach* (Harlow, UK: Financial Times Prentice Hall, 2003).

253  *Cloclo: La fabuleuse histoire de Claude François*, directed by Florent-Emilio Siri, 2012.

254  Survey conducted on February 6, 2000, cited in Donald Sassoon, *Mona Lisa: The History of the World's Most Famous Painting* (London: HarperCollins, 2009).

255  Ibid.

256  Ibid.

257  Ibid.

258  Sebastiaan, *Mysteries of Paris*, pp. 39–40; Jeremy Grange, "Resusci Anne and L'Inconnue: The Mona Lisa of the Seine," *BBC News Magazine*, October 16, 2013, http://www.bbc.com /news/magazine-24534069.

259  Chris Johnston, "Paul Gauguin's *When Will You Marry Me?* becomes most expensive artwork ever," *Guardian*, February 7, 2015, http://www.theguardian.com/artanddesign/2015/feb/07 /paul-gauguins-when-will-you-marry-becomes-most -expensive-artwork-ever.

260  Paul de Vaublanc, "Pourquoi est-il interdit d'appeler son cochon Napoléon?" *France 5*, February 8, 2013, http://www .france5.fr/emissions/c-a-dire/diffusions/08-02-2013_29899; also *Huffington Post*, January 23, 2012.

261  Owen Connelly, *Blundering to Glory: Napoleon's Military Campaigns* (Lanham, MD: Rowman & Littlefield, 2006), footnote, p. 7; Nic Fleming, "Short man syndrome is not just a tall story," *Telegraph*, March 13, 2008.

262  "Top 5 most expensive antique weapons," *Paul Fraser Collectibles*, January 6, 2014, https://www.justcollecting.com/mis cellania/top-5-most-expensive-antique-weapons.

263  Sarah Griffiths, "Could this wallpaper prove that Napoleon was murdered?" *Daily Mail*, March 6, 2014, http://www .dailymail.co.uk /sciencetech /article-2574655/Could -wallpaper-prove-Napoleon-MURDERED-D-cor-laced-toxic -arsenic-goes-auction.html.

264  Lockyer, *Last Words of Saints and Sinners*.

265  French government official bulletin for tourists.

266 Lorenz Schröter, *The Little Book of the Sea: Food and Drink* (London: Granta Books, 2009).

267 "The most visited cities: Shift Ranking of February 6," *Euromonitor International/Deutsche Welle,* February 6, 2015, http://www.dw.com/en/the-most-visited-cities-shift-ranking-of-february-6/a-18241426.

268 Jamie Cox Robertson, *A Literary Paris: Hemingway, Colette, Sedaris, and Others on the Uncommon Lure of the City of Light* (Avon, MA: Adams Media, 2010).

269 "The world's top bike-sharing cities: Shift Ranking of August 29," *The Bike-Sharing World Map/Deutsche Welle,* August 29, 2014, http://www.dw.com/en/the-worlds-top-bike-sharing-cities-shift-ranking-of-august-29/a-17887386.

270 "Les touristes japonais victimes du 'syndrome de Paris,'" *Le Parisien,* May 25, 2007, http://www.leparisien.fr/societe/les-touristes-japonais-victimes-du-syndrome-de-paris-25-05-2007-2008062610.php.

271 Robert J. Campbell, *Campbell's Psychiatric Dictionary,* 9th ed. (New York: Oxford University Press, 2009).

272 Dean MacCannell, *The Ethics of Sightseeing* (Berkeley: University of California Press, 2011).

273 Thomas Strentz, *Psychological Aspects of Crisis Negotiation,* 2nd ed. (Boca Raton, FL: CRC Press, 2012).

274 Dan Burstein and Arne De Keijzer, eds., *Secrets of Inferno: In the Footsteps of Dante and Dan Brown* (Stamford, CT: The Story Plant, 2013).

275 *Le Figaro,* October 3, 2012.

276 Glenday, *Guinness World Records, 2015.*

277 Lansky, *The Titanic Awards.*

278 Mairie de Paris.

279 Charles Cotolendi, *Saint-Evremoniana: Ou Recueil de diverses piéces curieuses* (Amsterdam: Chez Pierre Mortier, 1701), p. 292.

280  Michael B. Miller, *The Bon Marché: Bourgeois Culture and the Department Store, 1869–1920* (Princeton, NJ: Princeton University Press, 1994).

281  Eatwell, *They Eat Horses, Don't They?*

282  Paris infographic at SmarterParis.com, http://www.smarterparis .com/infographic-paris-in-figures/.

283  Ibid.

284  Tilar J. Mazzeo, *The Secret of Chanel No. 5* (New York: HarperCollins, 2010).

285  "Shalimar," on the Guerlain company's Web site, www.guerlain .com.

286  Wendy Bracat, "Parfums préférés des Français: Dior et Paco Rabanne restent en tête," *Le Huffington Post*, January 31, 2014, http://www.huffingtonpost.fr/2014/01/31/parfums-preferes -francais-dior-paco-rabanne_n_4701730.html.

287  Frédéric Lewino and Gwendoline Dos Santos, "16 février 1899. Le Président Félix Faure succombe à une fellation au palais de l'Élysée," *Le Point*, February 16, 2012, http://www .lepoint.fr/c-est-arrive-aujourd-hui/1899-une-fellation -presidentielle-a-l-elysee-16-02-2012-1431920_494.php; Victor Garcia, "Ces grands noms de l'Histoire sont morts dans des conditions improbables," *L'Express,* November 19, 2014, https://plus.google.com/+L-Express/posts/NTERNoYpwM6.

288  Alexander Lee, "The French Presidency: A School for Scandal," *History Today,* January 27, 2014, http://www.historytoday .com/blog/2014/01/french-presidency-school-scandal.

289  Christian Plume and Pierre Démaret, *Target de Gaulle: The True Story of the 31 Attempts on the Life of the French President* (London: Secker & Warburg, 1974).

290  Antonia Fraser, *Marie Antoinette* (London: Phoenix/Orion, 2001); Francine du Plessix Gray, "The Child Queen," *New Yorker*, August 7, 2000, http://www.newyorker.com/magazine /2000/08/07/the-child-queen.

291 Letcher, *Eccentric France.*

292 Will Bashor, *Marie-Antoinette's Head: The Royal Hairdresser, the Queen, and the Revolution* (Guilford, CT: Lyons Press/Globe Pequot Press, 2013); Will Bashor, "Marie Antoinette's Craziest, Most Epic Hairstyles," *Huffington Post,* October 16, 2013, http://www.huffingtonpost.com/will-bashor/marie -antoinettes-crazies_b_4109620.html.

293 Kathryn Lasky, *Marie Antoinette: Princess of Versailles, Austria-France, 1769* (New York: Scholastic Inc., 2000); Bisbort, *Famous Last Words.*

294 Samuel Prescott Hildreth, *Pioneer History* (District of Ohio: H. W. Derby & Co., 1848).

295 Ian Crofton, *A Curious History of Food and Drink* (London: Quercus, 2013).

296 Article R. 4228-20 of the French Employment Code.

297 Paris Police Ordinance, 1893.

298 Leo Wilkinson, "France breathalyser fine dropped," *Telegraph,* February 19, 2013, http://www.telegraph.co.uk /motoring/road-safety/9880120/France-breathalyser-fine -dropped.html.

299 "Le bêtisier des lois françaises," *Planet.fr,* January 26, 2011, http://www.planet.fr/dossiers-de-la-redaction-le-betisier-des -lois-francaises.48974.1466.html.

300 "Un maire prend un arrêté: c'est la politesse ou la porte," *Le Point,* November 28, 2012, http://www.lepoint.fr/insolite/un -maire-prend-un-arrete-c-est-la-politesse-ou-la-porte-28-11 -2012-1534852_48.php.

301 J. B. Bury, *The Cambridge Medieval History,* vol. 3 (Plantagenet Publishing, 2011); John Ardagh, ed., *The Penguin Guide to France* (New York: Viking, 1985).

302 *Oxford English Dictionary; Le Grand Robert: Langue française.*

303 "Laïcité en France," http://www.lemondepolitique.fr/culture /laicite-en-france.

304   *The Tablet*, August 19, 2006, www.thetablet.co.org.

305   "Paris city hall will not honour Scientologist Cruise," *World Wide Religious News, AFP*, July 12, 2005, http://www.expatica .com/fr/news/Paris-city-hall-will-not-honour-Scientologist -Cruise_130868.html.

306   "EU countries with the biggest Muslim population: Shift Ranking of January 28," *PewResearch/Deutsche Welle*, January 28, 2015, http://www.dw.com/en/eu-countries-with-the-biggest -muslim-population-shift-ranking-of-januar-28/a-18221926.

307   Robert Arp, ed., *1001 Ideas That Changed the Way We Think* (New York: Atria Books/Simon & Schuster, 2013).

308   Daniel Rogov, *Rogues, Writers and Whores: Dining with the Rich and Infamous* (London: Toby Press, 2007).

309   Eatwell, *They Eat Horses, Don't They?*

310   Rogov, *Rogues, Writers and Whores*.

311   Kenneth Clark, *Civilisation: A Personal View* (London: John Murray/Hodder & Stoughton, 1969; Kindle reissue, 2015).

312   Ken Alder, *The Measure of All Things: The Seven-Year Odyssey and Hidden Error that Transformed the World* (New York: Free Press, 2002); Peter McPhee, *The French Revolution, 1789–1799* (Oxford, UK: Oxford University Press, 2002).

313   *Le Grand Robert: Langue française*; *Oxford English Dictionary*.

314   Thomas Bradford et al., *Encyclopaedia Americana* (1851); "Récit fait par M. Drouet, maître de poste à Ste Menehould, de la manière dont il a reconnu le Roi, et a été cause de son arrestation à Varennes: honneurs rendus à ce citoyen et à deux de ses camarades," Collection: Les archives de la Révolution française, Bibliothèque National de France.

315   Fred S. Kleiner, *Gardner's Art through the Ages: The Western Perspective* (Boston: Wadsworth Publishing, 2013); Christopher John Murray, ed., *Encyclopedia of the Romantic Era, 1760–1850* (New York: Fitzroy Dearborn/Taylor & Francis Books, 2004).

316   2012 Skyscanner survey reported in Andrew Bender, "The World's Rudest Nations For Travelers," *Forbes*, April 3, 2012.

317   Katy Hastings, "New Mr Men character is French and Rude," *Telegraph*, February 10, 2008, http://www.telegraph.co.uk/news /uknews/1578209/New-Mr-Men-character-is-French-and -rude.html.

318   Cécile Ernst, *Bonjour madame, merci monsieur* (Paris: Éditions Jean-Claude Lattès, 2011).

319   *Le Grand Robert: Langue française*; *Oxford English Dictionary*.

320   "Cantine scolaire au collège et au lycée," official site of the French government at http://vosdroits.service-public.fr, April 13, 2015.

321   "Moins de sel et de ketchup au menu des cantines scolaires," *Le Monde*, October 3, 2011, http://www.lemonde.fr/societe /article/2011/10/03/une-plus-grande-variete-alimentaire-dans -les-cantines-scolaires_1581260_3224.html.

322   "Vatican criticizes condom machines in Rome school," *USA Today*, March 11, 2010, http://usatoday30.usatoday.com/news /religion/2010-03-11-Vatican_N.htm.

323   Mary Roach, *Bonk: The Curious Coupling of Science and Sex* (New York: W. W. Norton & Company, 2009).

324   Louis Crompton, *Homosexuality and Civilization* (Cambridge, MA: Harvard University Press, 2003).

325   Sean Thomas, "Dirty Bertie's seat of pleasure," *Times*, January 17, 2004, http://www.thetimes.co.uk/tto/arts/article2412867.ece.

326   Eatwell, *They Eat Horses, Don't They?*

327   Deidre Bair, interview by Scott Simon, "Anais Nin Husband, Rupert Pole Dies in L.A.," NPR News Weekend Edition, July 29, 2006, http://www.npr.org/templates/story/story.php ?storyId=5591676; Anaïs Nin, *The Diary of Anaïs Nin, 1931– 1934*, vol. 1 (Boston: Houghton Mifflin Harcourt, 1966).

328   Green, *Green's Dictionary of Slang*.

329   Roach, *Bonk*.

330   Geraldine Bedell, "I wrote the story of O," *Guardian*, July 25,

2004, http://www.theguardian.com/books/2004/jul/25/fiction
.features3.

331  Toni Bentley, "The Thin End of the Whip," *Vanity Fair*, February 2014, http://www.vanityfair.com/culture/2014/02/cathe
rine-robbe-grillet-french-dominatrix.

332  Report of an address by Jimmy Wales, founder of Wikipedia, to the 2009 Symbian Exchange and Exposition, APC, November 24, 2009.

333  "Consommation d'escargots en France," *Planetoscope.fr*, http://www.planetoscope.com/restauration/1339-consommation-d
-escargots-en-france.html.

334  "Escargot: une industrie ralentie par la sécheresse," *Les Marchés (l'agroalimentaire au quotidien)*, June 9, 2011, http://www
.fldhebdo.fr/escargot-une-industrie-ralentie-par-la-s-cheresse
-art306354-2388.html.

335  *Larousse Cuisine.*

336  Cited in De Vaublanc, *Plage interdite aux éléphants*, p. 12.

337  J. Barbary de Langlade, *Maxim's: cent ans de vie parisienne* (Paris: Robert Laffont, 1990).

338  Eatwell, *They Eat Horses, Don't They?*

339  Châteauneuf-du-Pape bylaw of 1954.

340  Letcher, *Eccentric France.*

341  Todd Van Luling, "8 Things You Didn't Know About the Artist Vincent Van Gogh," *Huffington Post*, November 21, 2014; Whitney, "Jeanne Calment, World's Elder, Dies at 122."

342  PF Ptak Science Books/World War History Online.

343  Joseph Harriss, *The Eiffel Tower: Symbol of an Age* (London: Paul Elek, 1975), pp. 180–84.

344  Elaine Sciolino, "Heroic Tale of Holocaust, With a Twist," *New York Times*, October 3, 2011, http://www.nytimes.com/2011
/10/04/movies/how-a-paris-mosque-sheltered-jews-in-the
-holocaust.html?_r=0.

345  "Introduction to the history of the camp," Struthof camp

information at http://www.struthof.fr/en/the-kl-natzweiler /introduction-to-the-history-of-the-camp/.

346 Colin Randall, "General 'spared Paris by disobeying Fuhrer,'" *Telegraph*, August 24, 2004, http://www.telegraph.co.uk/news /worldnews/europe/france/1470087/General-spared-Paris-by -disobeying-Fuhrer.html.

347 Figures from the Californian Wine Institute for 2012.

348 "US overtakes France as world's biggest wine market," *BBC News*, May 13, 2014, http://www.bbc.com/news/business-27401458.

349 Bylaw of 1984, cited in De Vaublanc, *Plage interdite aux éléphants*, p. 143; Catherine Coroller, "Forts de leurs pouvoirs de police municipal, certains dépessant allégrement les bornes," *Libération*, August 14, 1998.

350 "VINS/COMMERCE EXTERIOR, Bilan 2011/due 1er janvier au 31 décembre," *FranceAgriMer*, p. 13.

351 Nicola Williams, et al., *France* (London: Lonely Planet, 2015).

352 Carey Polis, "World's Most Expensive Bottle of Wine? 2009 Chateau Margaux Retailing for $195,000," *Huffington Post*, October 15, 2013, http://www.huffingtonpost.com/2013/10/15 /worlds-most-expensive-wine_n_4101904.html.

353 George M. Taber, *Judgment of Paris: California vs. France and the Historic 1976 Paris Tasting That Revolutionized Wine* (New York: Scribner/Simon & Schuster, 2005).

354 Antonin Iommi-Amunategui, "Les dix vins les plus LOL de France," *Le Nouvel Observateur*, July 2, 2012, http://rue89 .nouvelobs.com/blog/no-wine-innocent/2012/07/02/les-dix -vins-les-plus-lol-de-france-227885; ibid., *La cuvée « fucks@ rkozy », vin potache et militant, se boit bien*, April 24, 2012.

355 Button and Oliver, *Wine—101 Truths, Myths and Legends*, Amusing Names No. 5.

356 Jones, *Word Drops*.

357 *Le Bottin Mondain*, French etiquette guide, http://www.bottin -mondain.fr/qui-sommes-nous/.

358 "Séries TV: Esprits criminels, The Mentalist ou NCIS, les préférées des Français," *Baromètre Promise Consulting Inc./Le Huffington Post*, September 19, 2012, http://www.huffington post.fr/2012/09/18/series-tv-france-esprits-criminels -mentalist-ncis_n_1893934.html.

359 Guillemette Faure, "Au déjeuner des best-sellers," *Le Magazine du Monde*, March 14, 2014, http://www.lemonde.fr/m-actu /article/2014/03/14/au-dejeuner-des-best-sellers_4382350 _4497186.html.

360 "Qatar removes Zidane headbutt statue from Corniche," *BBC News,* October 30, 2013, http://www.bbc.com/news/world -middle-east-24747919.

361 "50 Things . . . You Didn't Know About the World Cup," *Wall Street Journal*, April 29, 2015.

# Bibliography

Detailed information on sources is given with each fact and/ or curiosity, as it is noted.

However, for those wishing to explore the peculiarities of France and the French further, may I suggest the following reference books in particular:

Bisbort, Alan. *Famous Last Words: Apt Observations, Pleas, Curses, Benedictions, Sour Notes, Bons Mots and Insights from People on the Brink of Departure.* Rohnert Park, CA: London Pomegranate Communications, 2001.

*Brewer's Dictionary of Phrase and Fable,* 19th rev. ed. London: Hodder Education, 2012.

Button, Roddy and Mike Oliver. *Wine—101 Truths, Myths and Legends.* Clacton on Sea, UK: Apex Publishing Limited, 2013.

*CIA: The World Factbook: Europe: France.* Central Intelligence Agency, updated June 22, 2014.

Darnton, Robert. *The Great Cat Massacre and Other Episodes in French Cultural History.* New York: Basic Books, 2009.

De Prelle, Patricia, et al. *Le Guide de l'Étiquette de du Savoir-Vivre.* Brussels: Editions Racine, 2001.

De Vaublanc, Paul. *Plage interdite aux elephants . . . : et autres bizarreries du droit!.* 2nd ed. Levallois-Perret, France: Éditions Bréal, 2013.

Donald, Graeme. *Lies, Damned Lies and History*. Stroud, UK: History Press, 2009.

Eatwell, Piu Marie. *They Eat Horses, Don't They? The Truth about the French*. New York: Thomas Dunne/St. Martin's Press, 2014.

Green, Jonathon. *Green's Dictionary of Slang*. London: Chambers Harrap, 2012.

*Guinness World Records*, 2015.

Hannan, Martin. *Harvey Wallbangers and Tam O'Shanters: A Book of Eponyms*. London: Metro/John Blake Publishing, 2011.

Johnston, Cristina. *France and the Americas: Culture, Politics and History*. Bill Marshall, 2005.

Jones, Colin. *The Cambridge Illustrated History of France*. Cambridge, UK: Cambridge University Press, 1994.

Jones, Paul Anthony. *Word Drops: A Sprinkling of Linguistic Curiosities*. London: Elliott & Thompson, April 2015. Kindle edition.

Letcher, Piers. *Eccentric France*. Chalfont St. Peter, UK: Bradt Travel Guides, 2003.

Létourneau, Lucie and Fabio Pellegrino. *Recevoir et être reçu (Savoir-vivre et etiquette t. 1)*. Montreal: Les Editions LaLucia, 2013. Kindle edition.

Nadeau, Jean-Benoît and Julie Barlow. *The Story of French*. London: Portico, 2010.

Rogov, Daniel. *Rogues, Writers and Whores: Dining with the Rich and Famous*. London: Toby Press, 2007.

Sebastiaan, Father. *Mysteries of Paris*. New York: Bast Books, 2014.

Toklas, Alice B. *The Alice B. Toklas Cook Book*, 2nd ed. London: Serif, 1998.